The Quest *for* Health Reform
A Satirical History

Georges C. Benjamin, MD
Theodore M. Brown, PhD
Susan Ladwig, MPH
Elyse Berkman

American
Public Health
Association
www.aphabookstore.org

American Public Health Association
800 I Street, NW
Washington, DC 20001-3710
www.apha.org

Georges C. Benjamin, MD, FACP, FACEP (Emeritus), Executive Director
Howard Spivak, MD, Publications Board Liaison
Stacy Lyons, OD, Publications Board Liaison

Printed and bound in the United States of America
Production Editor: Teena Lucas
Typesetting: The Charlesworth Group
Cover Design: Alan Giarcanella
Printing and Binding: Victor Graphics, Baltimore, MD

Library of Congress Cataloging-in-Publication Data

The quest for health reform : a satirical history / by Georges C. Benjamin . . . [et al.].
    p. cm.
  Includes bibliographical references and index.
  ISBN 978-0-87553-020-8 (alk. paper)
1. Medical care--Political aspects--United States--History--Caricatures and cartoons. 2. Medical care--Political aspects--United States--Caricatures and cartoons. 3. Medical care--United States--History--Caricatures and cartoons. 4. Medical care--United States--Caricatures and cartoons. I. Benjamin, Georges.
  RA418.3.U6Q84 2013
  362.102'07--dc23
                        2012030069

Table of Contents

Foreword

Fair and impartial journalism will always have a special place in my heart… just not in my work.

If the role of a journalist is to hold up a mirror to society, the mirror an editorial cartoonist uses is like the ones you find in a carnival funhouse: a mirror that's warped by our own perspective and one that reflects an image distorted by our own biases.

You see, unlike most journalists, we cartoonists aren't held to the same standards of objectivity and impartiality. One part reporter and one part advocate, an editorial cartoonist isn't merely an observer of the public debate, but an active participant in it, as well. As such, I'm expected to present a point of view: to depict the world as I see it, and to campaign for a world I would like to see.

During my years in this business, there have been many causes I've consistently (some might say hopelessly) promoted. For over three decades now, I have lobbied with pen and ink for campaign finance reform, economic justice, environmentalism, civil rights and universal health care coverage. Looking down that list of issues, it's obvious that some have advanced more than others.

Although campaign finance reform and economic justice have both proven to be unmitigated disasters over the past thirty years and environmentalism has been a mixed bag over my adult life, the struggles for civil rights and health care reform have been, in my opinion, qualified success stories.

I say 'qualified' successes, because try as I might to see a glass as half-full, I just can't seem to ignore that it's still half-empty.

The gains we've made in the civil rights for gays and lesbians in recent years, for instance, have been a tremendous development and a source of great encouragement, but the nagging inequities that persist in other parts of our society are as glaring as the deficiency in a woman's paycheck or the racial proportions of our nation's prison population. In a country founded on the premise that all men are created equal, it's still obvious that some of us seem to depreciate a lot more than others.

Healthcare is a similar case. Although President Obama's 'Affordable Care Act' was a big step forward toward the ultimate goal of universal health care coverage in this country, it's still several strides short of the comprehensive plans offered in almost every other industrialized nation in the world.

I do take comfort in the fact that a qualified success is still a success, and even though 'Obamcare' might be less ambitious than the single-payer system that I would prefer, I have to remind myself that the half-full glass, in this particular case, used to be bone dry.

Shortcomings aside, I was proud to support the president's efforts and give him a lot of credit for all that he was able to accomplish. As this book will attest, many presidents before him (in far less political polarized times) tried, and failed, to pass similar attempts to reform our health care system. It was a tough fight and both the president and the plan got pretty bruised up in the process, but it's a good start and it will provide millions of Americans with the health care coverage that was previously either unaffordable or unattainable.

I can't point to many successful campaigns progressives have waged over my career as an editorial cartoonist. So, as grateful as I am for all the practical good these reforms will bring, I've got to say that I'm just as thankful for some tangible evidence that the good guys actually can win every once in a while.

Maybe there's hope for campaign finance reform yet.

Clay Bennett
Editorial Cartoonist
Chattanooga Times Free Press

Preface

This book was conceived during my sabbatical when I served as the Joan H. Tisch Distinguished Fellow in Public Health at Hunter College. This one-semester fellowship, located at Roosevelt House Public Policy Center in New York City, required that I accomplish a project that advances the public's health. Roosevelt House is the former double townhouse home of President Franklin Delano Roosevelt (FDR) and his family, including his mother, Sara. The idea that I spent time living in the home of one of our nation's most important presidents, one who was such an architect of our social safety net, still sends shivers through my bones. In fact, it was one evening while sitting in the second floor library, the place where FDR conceived Social Security, when I finalized the idea about what I wanted to do. The Affordable Care Act was in its earliest stages of implementation and I was concerned that people did not seem to understand what the benefits were, but, most importantly, I was often surprised to hear people refer to health reform as though it was a new idea. I thought we needed a new way to tell the story.

I am both a visual learner and a fan of political cartoons. During the health reform debate, there were numerous cartoons that I thought captured the issues better than the written word ever could. I could not wait to see them daily and, coupled with what I knew was occurring politically, often reacted with gut-busting laughter. I decided that this would be a great way to tell the health reform story, and the more I thought about it, the more I felt we should capture the entire 100-year quest, especially since many of the themes, falsehoods, and criticisms repeated themselves across the years. I kicked the idea around with Dr. Jonathan Fanton, the FDR Visiting Fellow and another fan of political cartoons, as well as several of the key staff at Roosevelt House. They thought it was an interesting idea and helped me identify a research assistant, Elyse Berkman, to aid in the cataloging and management of the cartoon database. Elyse has been a wonderful and competent addition to the effort. I knew my colleague from the American Public Health Association, Ted Brown, a medical historian at the University of Rochester, had significant experience presenting the history of health reform through the use of images and cartoons and asked him to join with me in this effort. He and his colleague, Susan Ladwig, from the University of Rochester Medical Center's Center for Ethics, Humanities, and Palliative Care, quickly joined the team. This has been an amazing collaborative effort of which we are all immensely proud. I hope you find this book as humorous and informative as we did.

Georges C. Benjamin, MD, FACP, FACEP (E), FNAPA, Hon FRSPH
Joan H. Tisch Distinguished Fellow in Public Health
Adjunct Professor, CUNY School of Public Health at Hunter College
Executive Director
American Public Health Association, Washington, D.C.

American Public Health Association's Pursuit of Health Reform

1800s

In the 1870's a young physician Stephen Smith was concerned with the lack of health and disease prevention in the United States. His frustrations with the government's inability to act led him to found the American Public Health Association.

Stephen Smith's deep distress made him a health reformer bringing others into the fold. His experiences resonated with cartoons of the time. In fact Dr. Smith appears on a front-page cartoon in *New York's Daily Graphic* of May 10, 1873, where his name is brandished as a weapon of health reform.

<u>1900's</u>

President Harry S. Truman speaking at the 1945 APHA annual convention.

"Ten years almost to the very day, on November 19, 1945, I sent a special message on Health to the Congress of the United States. This message, I believe was the first transmitted by a President dealing exclusively with the subject of health. I sent that message to Congress because this great nation was doing so little to safeguard its most precious asset, the health and well-being of its citizens."

<u>2000's</u>

APHA members advocating for health reform.

Acknowledgments

I would like to take this opportunity to thank Dr. Marion Nestle, a well known public health advocate and colleague for connecting us with Sara Thaves, founder of The Cartoonist Group. Sara quickly saw the benefit of the concept and a partnership was in the works; she has been such a joy to work with. I am extremely grateful for my colleagues Ted Brown, Elyse Berkman, and Susan Ladwig for all of their hard work and dedication while working on this project and the hard work of the American Public Health Association's publications department, Nina Tristani, Director of Publications, Teena Lucas, the head of book production, and a host of creative graphic designers who helped bring this to fruition. I dedicate this book to my wife Yvette and other family members who all benefit from health reform.

Georges C. Benjamin, MD, FACP, FACEP (E), FNAPA, Hon FRSPH
Joan H. Tisch Distinguished Fellow in Public Health
Adjunct Professor, CUNY School of Public Health at Hunter College
Executive Director
American Public Health Association, Washington, D.C.

I want to acknowledge Alan Unsworth, the rock star of reference librarians; Michael Brown, insightful reader and supportive colleague; and Corinne Sutter-Brown, my favorite political pundit and constitutional scholar, for their support and help with this effort.

Theodore M. Brown, PhD
Professor of History and of Community & Preventive Medicine
University of Rochester, Rochester, NY

Cartoons should be fun. Working on this book and these cartoons was indeed fun, and much more. In fact, it was a dream come true for me to help make the whole unwinding saga of health reform efforts, with all its ups and downs, more accessible to the general public. Besides my gratitude to Georges Benjamin, Elyse Berkman and Ted Brown, all of whom are so wonderfully easy to work with, I would like to thank all those folks I corralled to tell parts of this sad story, whether they wanted to hear it or not. I am particularly grateful to my family for listening.

Susan Ladwig, MPH
Center for Ethics, Humanities and Palliative Care
University of Rochester Medical Center, Rochester, NY

I would like to thank Roosevelt House, Dr. Georges Benjamin and everyone at the American Public Health Association for giving me the opportunity to work on this exciting project.

Elyse Berkman, MPA (Candidate)
Baruch College, School of Public Affairs, New York, NY

Introduction

Cartooning and National Health Reform

This book brings together two American political traditions – editorial cartooning as a medium for trenchant contemporary commentary and the long-standing effort to achieve universal national health reform. As early as the nineteenth century, caricatures and cartoons parodied the leading personalities and institutions in American politics, as seen in the image to the right from an 1877 cartoon by Thomas Nast. Nast was probably the most famous cartoonist of his day (he invented the Republican elephant as one of his creations for *Harper's Weekly* in 1874) and in many ways he popularized this emerging form of political commentary in the United States.

Courtesy of U.S. Senate Collection.

1

The tradition began with cartoonists such as Nast and expanded into the twentieth century. Later representatives of that tradition applied their irony-dipped pens to every area of American politics and policy. This book focuses on national health reform, as told through the vision of popular editorial cartoonists.

We concentrate on the past three decades, from President William Clinton's efforts to achieve universal health coverage in the early years of his administration to President Barack Obama's push for what became the Patient Protection and Affordable Care Act of 2010 and the pushback to those efforts after the Act was passed. President Obama was well aware how long the United States has struggled with the health reform issue. In a nationally televised speech to a joint session of Congress in September 2009 he said, "I am not the first president to take up this cause, but I am determined to be the last." Cartoonist Mike Luckovich captured some of the emotion and political significance of that moment in this cartoon.

Matt Wuerker drew us back another several decades in this cartoon by alluding to President Theodore Roosevelt's role in the long saga.

The cartoons by Luckovich and Wuerker are examples of what this book contains. It presents the struggles over health reform from the vantage point of political cartoonists. By doing so, it will make you smile, frown, and at times shudder in horror when you reflect on the political opportunities sometimes seized but all too often missed at critical moments in our history. Before shifting focus to the past three decades, we will first review the broad sweep of health reform efforts starting with President Theodore Roosevelt and ending just before President Clinton took office. This review will set the stage for the

close scrutiny of the last three decades by illustrating what came before and also identifying several of the key themes and recurrent political patterns that emerged over time. Thus, the political uses of fear, hope, selective memory,

and outright distortion will be seen as running threads in our health reform history.

Political cartoons play an important role in all of our chapters but in Chapters 1 and 2, unlike Chapters 3 through 6, we will also turn to

a few other historical documents and photographs to better illustrate our history. Starting with Chapter 3 our only illustrations will come from the rich, full world of Mike Luckovich, Matt Wuerker, and their colleagues in modern political cartooning.

National Health Reform: The Early Years

Courtesy of Cornell University Library.

Most Americans are unfamiliar with how long the nation has been working on health reform and some may even think this is an entirely new concept. The truth is that this quest for universal health care coverage has a long and complicated history spanning many years and several political parties. Although this book primarily focuses on the three decades from the early 1990s to the present, we will first set the stage for what happens later by looking at the long history of attempts to achieve national health reform.

The first national campaign came at the turn of the twentieth century and even predates Theodore Roosevelt's embrace of the cause in 1912. It was launched by a reform coalition called the American Association for Labor Legislation (AALL), which was founded in 1906 during the American Progressive era. It was an alliance of prominent political figures, academics, health professionals, and social leaders who all wanted to protect American workers from the worst dangers of rapid industrial development in a dramatically changing society. The labor legislation sought by AALL would provide certain protections against the worst abuses that workers faced, such as excessive hours of work at low pay, dangerous work environments, exploitative conditions for women and children, and the great uncertainties of a boom-and-bust economy in a competitive labor market fed by large numbers of recent immigrants desperately competing for jobs.

One of AALL's great triumphs was its successful campaign for workmen's compensation benefits which, beginning in 1910, were legislated state by state to provide partial replacement wages for workers injured on the job. Also high on the agenda was health insurance (initially called sickness insurance), which would likewise help replace lost wages, in this case for work missed because of illness or disability. AALL members looked across the Atlantic to Germany, England, and other European countries, which had already successfully begun to create safety nets to protect workers and their families from the cycles and crises that came with the modern industrial economy. Reformers feared that robust American workers would soon be worn down if they did not have a comparable protective umbrella of social benefits, including health insurance.

The AALL-led campaign achieved considerable popularity. The Progressive Party, on whose ticket former President Theodore Roosevelt ran in 1912 as a third-party alternative to the Democratic and Republican candidates, adopted a platform that included endorsement of AALL's agenda under the heading "social and industrial justice." Specifically, the Progressive platform called for "the protection of home life against the hazards of sickness, irregular employment and old age through the adoption of a system of social insurance adapted to American use."

Protected!

Courtesy of the Cornell University Library.

Although Roosevelt lost the election to Woodrow Wilson, the cause of national health insurance continued to be strongly supported in the 1910s by influential writers, journalists, social reformers, public health officials, leaders of academic medicine, and the leadership of the American Medical Association (AMA), the major professional organization of American physicians. Some major labor organizations also supported the cause. Women workers who were fighting hard and effectively for social and industrial justice as well as the right to vote were strong advocates.

Courtesy of Kheel Center for Labor-Management Documentation and Archives, Cornell School of Industrial Labor Relations.

But health insurance had powerful enemies too, with strong resistance coming from traditionally conservative and right-wing politicians, who did not think it was the government's responsibility under any circumstances to weaken American individualism and provide what they considered a character-softening safety net. Many in the medical profession were also opposed, as they were terrified of what they perceived to be a government takeover of medical practice and a loss of income. Some sectors of labor, which feared government paternalism, were hostile as was the commercial insurance industry, which worried about the loss of paying customers if the government ran the system. These opposition forces generated a steady stream of propaganda emphasizing the "socialistic" and "un-American" nature of national health insurance, and this propaganda stream deepened and widened in the spring of 1917 with the United States' entry into World War I and with it, the rapid demonization of everything German. Some of this anti-health reform propaganda–which labeled health insurance as "compulsory," "Germanic," "socialistic," and "un-American"was directly traceable to the commercial insurance industry that cynically manipulated labor spokespersons such as Sara Conboy, who in reality was an organizer for the United Textile Workers of America, and invented phony patriotic organizations (New York League for Americanism), whose offices were listed at the addresses of commercial insurance companies.

Advocacy for the national health reform cause became even more difficult after the Russian Revolution in late 1917. A Red Scare quickly took hold in the United States and continued into the 1920s. This put a pall over all progressive political activity and saw, among other things, the hasty trial and summary jailing of left-wing leaders and raids against "Bolshevik" aliens led by U.S. Attorney General A. Mitchell Palmer, which resulted in the 1919 deportation of 249 alleged "dangerous radicals" who, it was claimed, had brought anarchy and revolution to the United States.

Courtesy of the New York Tribune.

The Red Scare also resulted in the expulsion of progressive labor leaders from many unions, the exclusion of legally elected representatives from legislative bodies if they happened to be socialists, and a political climate of isolationism, xenophobia, and conformity expressed in the purging of school textbooks of "un-American" points of view. In this environment, would-be supporters of national health insurance mostly stayed nervously and quietly under cover for fear of being labeled revolutionaries, a term the American Medical Association (AMA) more and more frequently relied on in its fight against health reform, which it initially supported. In many ways they were "for it" before they were "against it."

The AMA continued its assaults throughout the 1920s and eventually targeted all forms of public health, even popular maternal and childcare programs, as "state medicine." This particular attack so infuriated some American pediatricians that they broke away from the AMA. Yet led by the _Journal of the American Medical Association_ (_JAMA_) editor Morris Fishbein, the AMA kept up its attacks on what it referred to as socialized medicine and now added another scare tactic: government-provided medical care would automatically become depersonalized and robotic.

Socialized Medicine
By Morris Fishbein
April 25, 1928 Vol. 126(3277)

…"The mechanization of medicine is an evil recognized by every physician as a menace to sound medical practice. Come what may, the intimate personal relationship of physician and patient is essential to complete relief of the patient's ills. Even the periodical physical examination is unsatisfactory when applied on an impersonal basis."…

…"State medicine might provide a standardized diagnosis and treatment for a standardized citizen; but it means the death of individualism, of humanitarianism, and of scientific practice. Until we become a nation of robots with interlocking, replaceable and standardized parts, there will be little need of completely standardized doctors."…

Courtesy of The Nation.
April 25, 1928. Vol. 126, Issue 3227.

In the 1930s, the AMA directed its attacks against anything even remotely like national health reform, and its campaign sometimes took bizarre turns. In late 1932, for example, a *JAMA* editorial attacked the Final Report of the Committee on the Costs of Medical Care (CCMC), a deliberately middle-of-the-road group which tentatively suggested local experiments in the financing and organization of medical care, *not* national health insurance. Nevertheless, *JAMA* claimed that CCMC's recommendations came from "forces representing … socialism and communism – inciting to revolution." A few years later, the AMA flexed its muscles again, this time to shape the Social Security Act of 1935, a key piece of President Franklin Roosevelt's New Deal legislation. The Social Security Act included modest funds for maternal and child health services, for crippled children, vocational rehabilitation, and public health services. In many ways this was the beginning of public health system support and reform as these federal funding streams became the basis of desperately needed state programs. But the Social Security Act as passed contained nothing directly relevant to national health insurance. There had been some discussion of health insurance issues in a preliminary administration report, but Roosevelt suppressed the report. The final Act offered provisions mostly for unemployment and old age insurance. The Roosevelt administration weighed many considerations in setting these priorities, but significantly among them was its fear, for very good reason, that inclusion of health insurance would provoke the outraged opposition of the AMA members, who would mobilize their allies in Congress – conservative Republicans and southern Democrats – and kill the entire bill.

President Franklin Roosevelt signs Social Security Act on August 14, 1935. © Bettmann/CORBIS.

The Roosevelt administration made another push for major health reform beginning in 1937, when the Social Security Act was firmly in place. The President authorized a new internal report on a possible national health program, which was completed in February 1938. The report recommended expansion of the child care and public health provisions already in Social Security and two new kinds of federal grants to states – for medical care of the poor and for health insurance for the general public. A National Health Conference in Washington, D.C. in the summer of 1938 was designed to build momentum for the latter two proposals but, once again, the AMA mobilized opposition and its congressional allies responded as expected. Reform-minded physicians fought back and a pitched battle ensued between the progressive and conservative wings of the medical profession.

When Doctors Disagree

Nevertheless, liberal Democratic Senator Robert Wagner of New York introduced a bill and, true to form, the AMA representatives called it "revolutionary" when they testified at scheduled hearings in May 1939. The bill died when it failed to receive substantial administration support.

AMA representatives appear at Wagner hearing on proposed health care bill in Washington, D.C., May 25, 1939. Dr. R.G. Leland (on right), Director of the Bureau of Medical Economics of the AMA, call the bill "revolutionary." Courtesy of the Library of Congress, Washington, D.C.

Despite legislative failure in Congress, the campaign for national health reform continued to build momentum. The cause now attracted many prestigious and high visibility advocates, such as Johns Hopkins historian of medicine Henry E. Sigerist, who was so famous and respected that he appeared on the cover of *Time* magazine. Sigerist also spoke at popular venues, where he argued the case for national reform with erudition and passion.

Courtesy of The Alan Mason Chesney Medical Archives of The John's Hopkins Medical Institutions. Reprinted by permission.

Many other leaders in academic medicine, the arts, the world of philanthropy, and the social sciences joined the crusade. But the opposition fought back with all its weapons to argue the contrary case. CBS Radio staged regular debates between Sigerist and the AMA's Fishbein on its popular radio show, "Town Hall of the Air," which reached millions of homes across the country.

In this climate, the Democrats led a charge for legislative enactment. During World War II, in 1943 Senator Wagner, along with cosponsors Senator James Murray of Montana and Representative John Dingell of Michigan, introduced an ambitious bill that included comprehensive health insurance and expanded support for the elderly. President Roosevelt also returned to the health insurance issue. In his January 1944 State of the Union message, he called for an "economic bill of rights," which would include a "right to adequate medical care" and a "right to adequate protection from the economic fears" of illness. But Roosevelt himself was too sick to follow through and died in April 1945. The Wagner-Murray-Dingell bill died too, even before it reached the floor of Congress.

2

The Middle Years of Health Reform

It fell to Harry Truman to become the first sitting president in our country's history to take up the cause of national health reform. A staunch New Deal Democrat, he had been Roosevelt's Vice President and became President on Roosevelt's death. He spoke out strongly for national health insurance, especially in a November 1945 message to Congress. But postwar conditions were not favorable. The country went through a turbulent reconversion to a peacetime economy and entered a period of unsettling labor disputes at the same time that it moved into a treacherous phase in

Courtesy of BACM Research.

foreign relations marked by the Cold War. All this was turned against Truman, whose calls for national health insurance were portrayed by his opponents as far more than the country could handle.

Within a few years, the political conditions for comprehensive reform were even less favorable. Just as after World War I, so too after World War II the country swung dramatically to the right and entered another era of Red Scare, this one in the form of McCarthyism, even more pervasive and intense than the one three decades earlier. McCarthyism was a political style dominated by smear tactics and "terror" relied on most notoriously by Senator Joseph McCarthy who often fabricated claims of "disloyalty" and "unAmericanism." Positive views the President's national health program was just what the ailing nation needed were countered by negative views that saw it as a "quack" intervention contributing to "political pollution" and "socialized medicine."

"The new brood?"

From Chicago Tribune, February 24, 1949 © 1949 by the Chicago Tribune. All rights reserved. Reprinted by permission.

Perhaps most notable in the postwar period was the deliberate use of red-baiting, McCarthyite tactics, and the manipulation of Cold War anxieties in the all-out mobilization against proposals for national health insurance. The AMA and its allies portrayed the Wagner-Murray-Dingell bills and the campaign for their enactment as parts of a subversive plot, engineered in the Kremlin, to sap the strength of America and make it vulnerable to communism.

Courtesy of Free Speech Radio News.

This lethal political environment contributed significantly to the melting away of organized labor's support for national health insurance in the late 1940s and early 1950s. In this climate, labor leaders decided to give up that politically damaging approach and shift instead to the more pragmatic promotion of collectively bargained, employment-based, commercially provided health insurance for American workers. This strategic political shift during the McCarthy era was a major reason for the creation in the United States of its unique system of employment-based and largely privately provided health insurance. This system spread rapidly in the 1950s, encouraged by the Eisenhower administration, which was adamantly opposed to socialized medicine and rewarded employers and employees for purchasing private insurance with substantial tax breaks. After a few years, however, the pitfalls of that system were evident. Health costs started to escalate, at first without many complaints from the insured population (workers and their immediate families). However, those escalated costs greatly affected the elderly and retired, who were *not* covered by employer-provided insurance as they had been during their working years. Growing recognition of the extent and severity of this problem fostered the rebirth of labor advocacy for national health insurance, now in a specific form targeted at retired workers 65 and older. This was the Medicare strategy, which by the later 1950s was increasingly promoted by policy leaders, liberal Democrats, organized labor, and the growing number of politically alert and mobilized older citizens. It was relatively easy to make the case for Medicare by focusing on the unmet medical needs of the elderly, who appeared sicker, poorer, and more deserving of sympathy and concern than any other group.

From The Tennessean, April 26, 1960 © 1960 by The Tennessean. All rights reserved. Reprinted by permission.

John F. Kennedy ran for President in 1960 with a prominent pro-Medicare plan on his platform, but his narrow electoral victory did not assure easy congressional passage. In fact, many in Congress were deeply resistant and the familiar, formidable alliance of conservative Republicans and Southern Democrats kept the measure bottled up in committee.

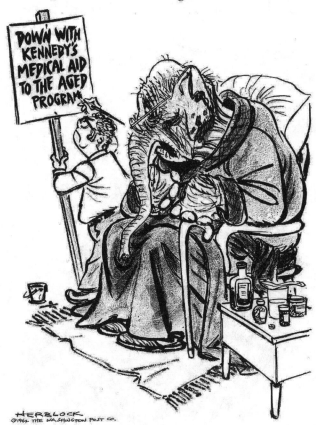

"Son, Let's Not Be Too Dogmatic About This"

Kennedy tried to shore up backing for the bill by rallying Medicare's most ardent supporters – organized labor, the elderly, and various progressive organizations like the National Association of Social Workers. Stacked against them were not only the AMA crying "socialized medicine" once again, but also the American Hospital Association, the National Association of Manufacturers, the Chamber of Commerce, and the American Legion. In a 1961 vinyl recording promoted by the AMA, actor Ronald Reagan, a Democrat at that time, urged the public to stand against socialized medicine.

Courtesy of the American Medical Association Archives.

Different this time was the administration's willingness to challenge the AMA aggressively, a stance made easier by the widespread criticism now directed at the AMA for its long-standing opposition to reform as well as by a growing view that the organization was out of touch, dyspeptic, and, despite its rhetoric, exclusively self-interested.

Some criticism came of the AMA from prestigious leaders of the medical profession itself, and some of it came from senior citizens.

Courtesy of The Detroit News.
Reprinted by permission.

In the very unusual circumstances following in the wake of Kennedy's assassination in November 1963 and a subsequent national dedication to the fallen president's goals, the Democrats won huge majorities in the 1964 congressional election. Lyndon Johnson swept triumphantly into office in a landslide victory. Johnson, like Truman before him, was a staunch New Deal Democrat who saw the merits of Medicare and was willing to push hard for the measure by using all the political skills he had learned in his three decades in Congress. He was also helped by the Civil Rights movement, which he likewise came to support, because leaders like Martin Luther King, Jr. saw Medicare through the lens of social justice. At the same time, African-American leaders realized that Medicare could be used strategically as carrot and stick to help desegregate America's hospitals, which strengthened their support for the Medicare cause. Other health groups like the American Public Health Association (APHA) and the American Nurses Association (ANA) were also strong advocates for Medicare and as support built for the program Republican politicians and even the AMA offered their own versions of the legislation.

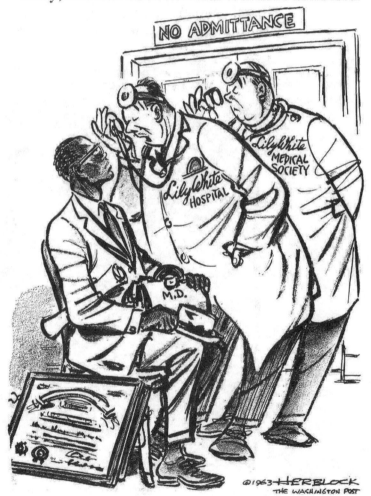

"Sorry, But You Have An Incurable Skin Condition"

Medicare was ultimately passed by Congress in 1965 with strong bipartisan support. Closely tied to Social Security and administered as a uniform federal program of earned entitlement, Medicare had a built-in and highly mobilized constituency of the elderly. In the final legislative maneuverings it became linked to Medicaid, a state-based and means-tested program of medical care for the poor, which had originally been promoted by conservatives as an alternative to Medicare. Even as passed in 1965 in the same legislative package as Medicare, Medicaid remained vulnerable because it lacked an organized political constituency and was seen as a charity program closely tied to state-based welfare policy. Brushing aside these complexities, President Johnson chose to sign the measure in the presence of former President Truman in a triumphal moment rich in historical and symbolic significance.

President Lyndon Johnson signs Medicare bill, with Harry Truman looking on, July 30, 1965. Courtesy of The Lyndon Baines Johnson Library & Museum, Austin, Texas.

Soon after Medicare passed, a campaign was launched to extend and generalize national health insurance to the entire population. Thus universal health reform returned to the political stage and immediately gained advocates in organized labor, various progressive organizations, and liberal political circles. By the late 1960s liberal Democratic Senator from Massachusetts Edward Kennedy and his allies had crafted legislation to create a universal national health insurance program in the United States.

The national health insurance movement expanded quickly in the early seventies, with a proliferation of liberal, moderate, and conservative proposals, all aiming to achieve universal, across-the-age spectrum coverage. Varying from single-payer Medicare-style proposals to employer mandates to tax credits to incentivize the purchase of commercial insurance, the proposals now under active debate reflected the differing political views of their proponents. Even Republican President Nixon and the AMA offered proposals, the former to some extent in an attempt to redirect attention from the growing Watergate scandal and the latter in the hopes of shaping to its liking what was assumed to be an inevitable reality. The Nixon plan proposed universal coverage with a plan that had employers picking up 65% of the costs. While it was touted as universal coverage, employer participation was voluntary. By 1974, a Democratic-Republican compromise seemed achievable, but then Nixon was consumed by the Watergate scandal and forced to resign. Tensions over priorities and approaches divided and deflected the Democrats.

"ROSALYNN, IT'S HIM AGAIN"

©1979 HERBLOCK

 An even larger problem loomed when the economy neared a crisis with "stagflation" – simultaneous stagnant economic growth and rapidly rising inflation. The economic woes deepened already growing anxieties about the excessive costs of health care, where inflation considerably outpaced growth of the economy in general. By the mid-seventies, health care costs and how to contain them displaced expansion of access as the central problem in health policy, and some former supporters of health reform now vowed to get rising costs under control first before moving on to universalizing benefits. In 1976 Jimmy Carter was elected President on the Democratic ticket, promising reform, but he was a very different and far more conservative Democrat than Kennedy. He regarded other domestic issues as higher priority and instead tried to put the brakes on what was left of the movement toward national health reform, some say because of a stagnant economy. Senator Kennedy persisted in trying to lead the charge, much to President Carter's dismay.

By the late seventies, there was widespread belief that liberal policies and regulatory reforms had failed to contain health care costs and that government initiatives in general were unable to lead the country forward. The deregulation of significant parts of the economy and the impetus towards privatization and free-market principles gained considerable popularity. This shift in national mood was propelled forward by Ronald Reagan in his 1980 presidential campaign. His election ushered in an era of "Reaganomics" and for eight years his administration did everything it could to unleash what it perceived to be the creative power of the unrestrained market while cutting as much of the social safety net (welfare) as it could get away with. Medicaid and other Great Society programs introduced in the sixties were slashed with a heavy axe, but Medicare survived primarily because of labor support and its strong and well-organized political base of mobilized elderly voters.

In this environment, no one dreamed of national health reform and in 1980 and 1984 the Democrats dropped that plank from their presidential platform.

During the Reagan era, health costs continued to rise and were coupled with a downturn in health outcomes leading to new cries for national health reform. Cuts in social programs were the norm and for the first time in decades, mortality rates stopped dropping while racial disparities in health indicators like adult and infant mortality and life expectancy grew significantly. By the mid-1980s, a shift in national mood led to the restoration of the Democrats to a majority in both the Senate and the House of Representatives. Soon afterward, Medicaid restoration and then expansion began with a particular focus on pregnant women and children, including the development of early versions of what would later become the State Children's Health Insurance Program (SCHIP).

Other health problems also gained increasing attention in the late 1980s. The growing number of those without health insurance, especially among the working poor, emerged as a major national concern as did the continued, seemingly unrestrained escalation of health care costs. This latter problem had a surprising impact on the middle and working classes because, even while covered by employer-provided commercial health insurance, they paid a rapidly rising share of health insurance premiums and out-of-pocket expenses (deductibles and co-pays) as employers tried to contain their own costs by shifting costs back to their employees.

Health Maintenance Organizations (HMOs), which the Nixon administration had tried to promote in the seventies with limited success, now became a much larger presence on the health landscape. Employers turned to these managed care organizations in an attempt to control their health care costs, but their unhappy employees found that the HMOs were often run with aggressive administrative hands by private national chains that profited by limiting access to care and cutting benefits. In this environment, two interesting developments took place: (1) a group of liberal physicians founded the Physicians for a National Health Program (PNHP) as an energetic and quickly influential single-payer advocacy group and (2) Jesse Jackson ran for the 1988 Democratic presidential nomination on a strong health reform and single-payer platform.

Jesse Jackson on the campaign trail in Philadelphia, 1988. Courtesy of Harvey Finkle.

Although Jackson did not win the Democratic nomination, his effective advocacy of the health reform issue at the Democratic National Convention pushed the party to return to its national health reform commitment and to choose as its presidential nominee then Massachusetts Governor Michael Dukakis, who had strong health reform credentials. Dukakis lost the election to George H.W. Bush, but Bush's avoidance of the health reform issue during his campaign and throughout most of his presidency failed to contain the gathering political momentum for comprehensive national health reform.

In May 1991 the AMA, in an evolution of its longstanding anti-reform position, began refocusing on the growing problem of the uninsured. Elsewhere the problem of runaway costs was on the minds of the insured and their employers. National health reform was again becoming a hot-button issue on the national political scene.

3

The Debate Returns with a Vengeance

Candorville

By the early 1990s obtaining affordable health insurance had again become an embarrassing national crisis.

HEALTH COVERAGE

Problems with health insurance were now a widespread middle class concern, and politicians were starting to comprehend that the U.S. health care system was grossly deficient in several ways. It not only failed to cover growing millions of people, but those who were covered by insurance were increasingly burdened by rapidly escalating costs. Many were alarmed by the administrative inefficiencies resulting from the country's complex multipayer claims and reimbursement system.

As reform proposals emerged, they varied along a spectrum that stretched from conservative advocacy for individual insurance mandates and vouchers for the poor (to help them purchase commercial insurance) to liberal support for a Canadian-style, government oversight of a single-payer system.

No simple consensus developed about the specifics of reform, and the proliferation of proposals led to confusion, suspicion, and, ultimately, stalemate.

During the 1992 presidential election campaign, candidate Bill Clinton began with a "play-or-pay" proposal by which employers either provided health insurance for their employees ("play") or paid into a fund that would provide public insurance for the otherwise uninsured ("pay"). Over the course of his campaign, Clinton's ideas gradually shifted to a version of

the managed competition proposal first advanced by Stanford economist Alain Enthoven and the Jackson Hole group of elite policy advocates, which received prominent endorsement by the editors of the *New York Times* and other media leaders. Many feared that, whatever specific plan Clinton supported, national health reform would be enormously expensive to implement.

After electoral victory in November and soon after his inauguration in January 1993, Clinton appointed a health reform Task Force chaired by First Lady Hillary Clinton and run by policy expert Ira Magaziner. The Task Force was supposed to sort through the various options and work out the specifics for implementation of Clinton's managed competition scheme, but it never really achieved its goals. Instead, it drew considerable criticism for its perceived exclusiveness, secrecy, and excessive complexity, and it was considerably undercut by damaging leaks, political missteps, and public relations gaffes. The Task Force's process seemed to build staircases to nowhere.

The centerpiece of Clinton's reform plan, managed competition, was intended to be the perfect strategic compromise between market-driven and government-overseen approaches to health reform, but instead of winning friends from all sides as he anticipated, the overall proposal generally deepened hostility and suspicion. Some of it came from those who understandably confused "managed competition" with "managed care," the latter having become deeply unpopular by the 1990s.

Clinton zig-zagged politically trying to solve specific problems and answer criticisms. While the proponents of reform battled over principles and priorities, opponents were able to take advantage of the disarray among the Democrats and moderate Republicans. Democrats did not unite and wholeheartedly embrace the plan, while conservatives, libertarians, and vested interests actively opposed it. As the battles proceeded, health reform seemed increasingly unlikely to emerge from its amphibian state.

YOU HAVE TO EXPECT SOME CUTBACKS WITH THE CLINTON HEALTH PLAN...

Opposition effectively eroded earlier support from business, labor, and health industry groups and rallied right-wing grassroots antagonism through strategic use of talk radio and effective media campaigns, most famously the "Harry and Louise" commercials sponsored by the Health Insurance Association of America, which parodied the excessive complexity of managed competition. The Clinton plan was viewed more and more as absurd.

By late 1993, hard-line conservative Republicans were already planning a campaign for the 1994 midterm Congressional elections focused on a demonization of the Clinton health reform proposal. Republicans strategists realized that killing healthcare reform and delegitimizing the very effort in an increasingly partisan political climate was a good political strategy for winning Congressional seats.

While Democrats tried to overcome their miscues,
possibilities for comprehensive reform expired.

However, even after their midterm victory in 1994,
the Republicans could not repeal Medicare and
other still-popular government health programs.

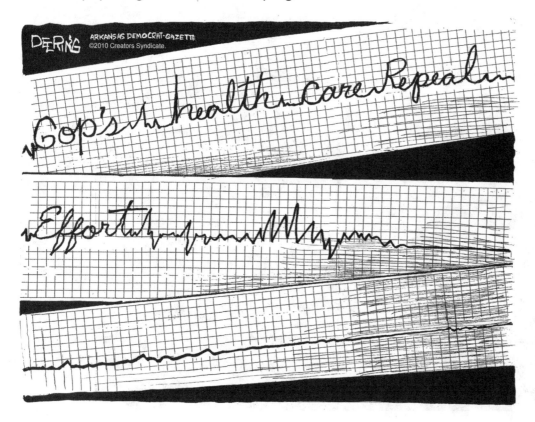

In many eyes, they simply became the party of "We Don't Care."

Yet, in the late 1990s the Democrats and Republicans were able to agree on some notable incremental health reforms. The Health Insurance Portability and Accountability Act (HIPAA), originally cosponsored by Democratic Senator Ted Kennedy and Republican Nancy Kassebaum, passed in the Senate by a 98-0 vote and was enacted in August 1996. HIPAA achieved modest success by limiting restrictions that group health plans could place on benefits for preexisting conditions and is best remembered for its patient privacy stipulations.

The State Children's Health Insurance Program (SCHIP) was a more significant success. Cosponsored by Kennedy and Republican Senator Orrin Hatch and supported by the Clinton Administration as well as by groups ranging from the Children's Defense Fund to the Girl Scouts, SCHIP became law in August 1997. With revenues from an increased federal tax on cigarettes as well as rising federal resources coming from economic growth, SCHIP was used to cover children in families with incomes up to twice the federal poverty level and was implemented in all states except Arizona.

"An ounce of prevention *was* worth a pound of cure, but that was before Medicare."

Because of confidence built on a growing budget surplus and bipartisan cooperation, the climate for incremental health reform was beginning to look so promising in the late 1990s that Clinton proposed a Medicare prescription drug benefit. Drug costs were now becoming an increasingly large part of Medicare costs.

These measures were blocked by the health care industry and conservative politicians, but they resurfaced in Al Gore's 2000 presidential campaign and in George W. Bush's "me too" response.

In the 2000 election, the Republicans gained control not only of Congress but also of the White House for the first time since the Eisenhower years, so prospects for comprehensive reform dimmed substantially. But the pharmaceutical industry withdrew its opposition to a Medicare drug benefit, realizing that a friendly administration would promote a bill crafted to its liking. President Bush and the Republicans pushed their version of the measure, which would help the drug companies reap windfall profits, after the 2002 midterm election and with an eye on the 2004 presidential campaign.

The Senate Finance Committee approved a bipartisan bill which the Senate passed by more than a three-quarters majority. It was widely suspected that the Senate was bowing to the pressure of health industry lobbyists.

The political battle was much more intense in the House, with the legislation squeaking through there by a 220 to 215 majority.

The Medicare Modernization Act of 2003 (MMA) had glaring gaps, the most famous of which was the "donut hole," the coverage gap of prescription drug expenses that Medicare beneficiaries still had to pay for out of pocket.

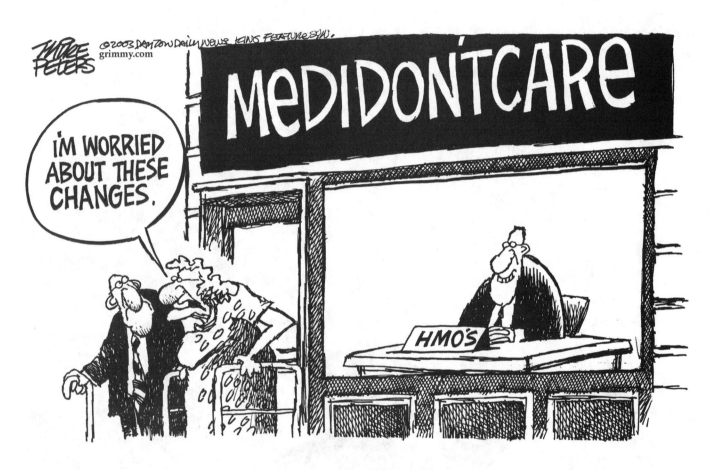

MMA also pushed in the direction of the privatization of Medicare by giving private insurance companies a large role in the administration of the new drug benefit.

More significantly, MMA prohibited the government from using its collective purchasing power to negotiate directly with pharmaceutical companies over drug prices. This meant that many senior citizens looked to Canada, where the government's purchasing leverage kept the prices of drugs at reasonable levels.

Many were angered by the huge profits that were guaranteed to the pharmaceutical industry, and public resentment increased with the chaotic initial implementation of the drug benefit in January 2006. Even the stock figures "Harry and Louise," who were widely used by the health insurance industry in 1993 to help derail Clinton health reform, were called back into play.

Most anger was directed
at the suspicion of
profit-driven industry
manipulation and the
tortuous complexity of
the new regulations.

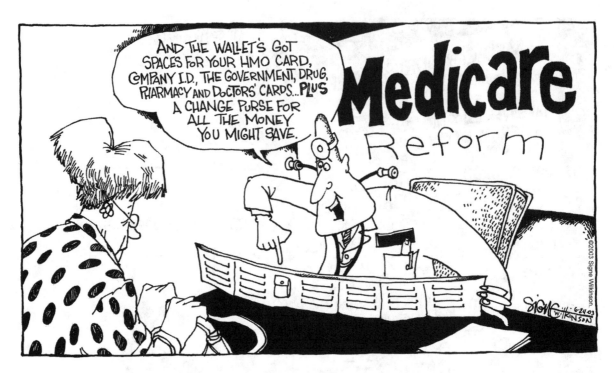

Some analysts suggested that the Republicans lost Congress in November 2006 in large part because of anger over the MMA.

The Democrats retook the House and Senate in 2006, but although the increasingly unaffordable cost of health care was already an acute concern to the public and the policy community, they were unable to push through major reforms. Many thought that corporate interests and their political influence were major culprits.

Instead of pushing for reform, President Bush in 2007 vetoed reauthorization of the generally popular State Children's Health Insurance Program (SCHIP) despite widespread support for its extension and the fact that 17 Republican Senators voted along with the Democrats.

Bush argued without credible evidence that SCHIP was "crowding out" the private insurance coverage of children and was a step on the road to the government takeover of health care. His critics argued that other considerations also influenced his decision.

Many children were left without adequate coverage, and they were not the only ones.

4

Same Quest — Similar Critics

The massive and rapidly growing problems in the U.S. health care system were even more undeniable by the first decade of the twenty-first century.

The Institute of Medicine of the National Academy of Science was just one of many prestigious groups to point out that the largely uncontrolled increase of health care costs — far outpacing inflation, growth in national gross domestic product (GDP), and growth in personal incomes — was gobbling up America's resources and leading to rapidly growing numbers of the uninsured, the underinsured, personal bankruptcies, and devastating health outcomes. It was widely understood that something had to be done and that leaving things to right themselves by the market alone would be an inadequate response.

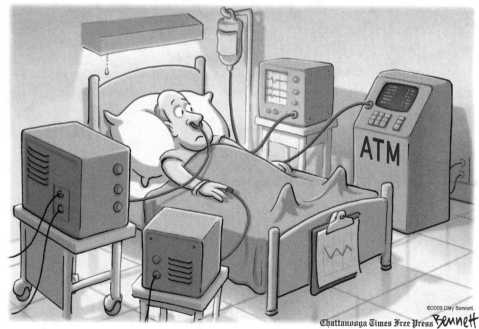

Data were rapidly accumulating about the United States' poor standing internationally in measures of health system performance. The World Health Organization released a widely read report that ranked the United States 37th (far below the top performer France) because of its relatively high mortality rate and low life expectancy, while it was off the charts in terms of per capita health care costs. In 2005, CDC researchers noted that the U.S. infant mortality rate was higher than the rates in most other developed countries and that the relative position of the United States compared with those of countries with better infant mortality rates appeared to be worsening.

59

The Physicians for a National Health Program (PNHP) used these data to bolster its growing campaign for universal, single-payer health care in the United States ("Medicare for All"), and picked up significant support from labor, professional, and religious organizations. But few understood what "single-payer" meant.

Yet awareness was growing that fear of a government takeover of health care was in many ways a deliberate scare tactic and an engineered deflection of attention from the real issue, which was the high-handed, deceptive, and often profit-driven behaviors of certain components of the commercial health industry.

In January 2003, the *American Journal of Public Health* (AJPH), the journal of the American Public Health Association, devoted an entire issue to "Rekindling Reform" and included an editorial by Senator Ted Kennedy in which he declared that the American health care system was in a crisis that worsened every year and was in urgent need of reform.

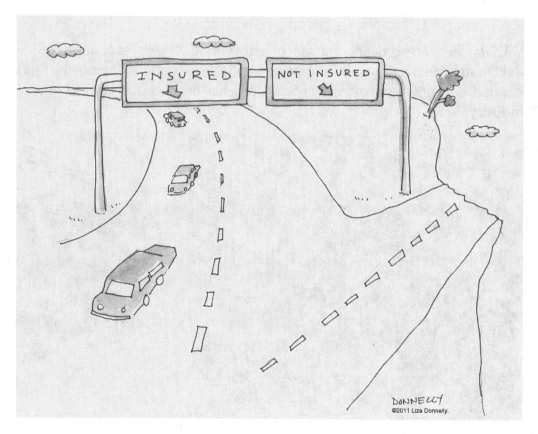

Kennedy ended his editorial by insisting that universal health insurance become a national priority, "so that the basic right to health care can finally become a reality for every American."

These powerful stimuli led to a response on the part of moderate policy leaders and political figures at the middle of the political spectrum, which took the form of an agenda of reforms

aimed at closing gaps in coverage and filling in missing pieces in the U.S. system. Critics saw this approach as a minimally invasive patchwork that failed to address the big issues head on.

'I know, let's compromise and build it out of twigs.'

This moderate approach was incremental rather than comprehensive and did not aim to achieve egalitarian universal access or outcome. Rather, this politically centrist approach aimed to ameliorate an increasingly horrendous situation without antagonizing large vested interests and the "protected public" covered by commercial insurance or Medicare.

Critics thought this approach inadequate, for obvious reasons.

One of the first steps on the path to incremental reform was taken by the Center for American Progress (CAP), a new policy research and advocacy organization founded in 2003 as a Democratic alternative to the conservative Heritage Foundation favored by the Republicans. In 2005, CAP deliberately steered clear of creating a new system and opted instead for a plan that would build on Medicaid and employer-based insurance for those under 65 by offering extended Medicaid for the poor and refundable tax credits for those in higher income brackets and by creating a national insurance exchange to sell commercial insurance to the uninsured.

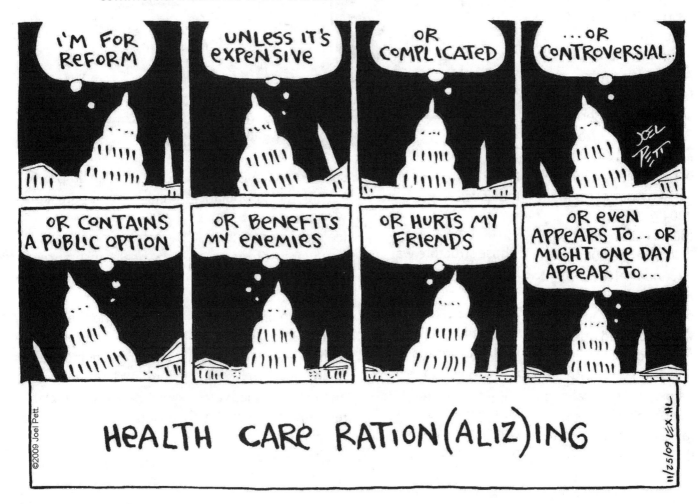

The Health Care Coalition for the Uninsured (HCCU), a collaborative effort of 16 national organizations including the American Association of Retired Persons (AARP), the American Academy of Family Physicians, the American Hospital Association, the AMA, American Health Insurance Plans, the APHA, Blue Cross and Blue Shield, Johnson & Johnson, Kaiser Permanente, Pfizer, and the U.S. Chamber of Commerce, began a consensus process in 2004 that led to more than a dozen meetings in 2005 and 2006. By January 18, 2007, HCCU announced its consensus proposal, which focused on the expansion of Medicaid and SCHIP for those below or slightly above the poverty level and tax credits to purchase private insurance for

those up to three times that level.

By this time a plan whose structure was basically parallel to CAP's and HCCU's proposals had already been implemented in Massachusetts under Governor Mitt Romney. This was the Massachusetts Plan which had won local bipartisan political

support and enjoyed considerable popularity with the state's business leaders, insurers, and provider institutions. The essential features of the plan were an expansion of Medicaid and SCHIP with subsidies and tax credits for low-income people, an individual mandate requiring all other state residents to purchase health insurance

coverage, an employer requirement to make a fair and reasonable contribution toward the health insurance coverage of their employees or pay a penalty, and the setting up of a health insurance exchange for individuals and small businesses to purchase commercial insurance.

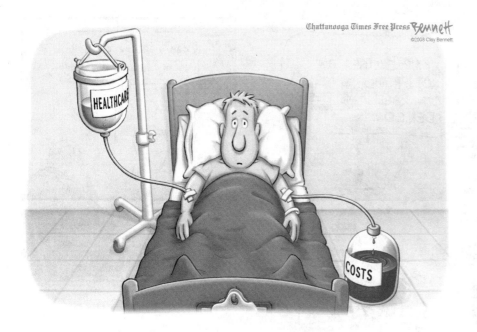

A 2012 assessment of Mass Health by the Kaiser Family Foundation demonstrated that the Massachusetts reforms had cut the number of uninsured about in half but did not slow the rate of growth of health care costs in the state, which clearly meant that the plan, as many had predicted at its start, produced mixed results.

Elsewhere in the United States the situation grew unremittingly dire, and public awareness that something was very wrong grew substantially.

In any case, many plans had begun to emerge on the national scene in 2007, although far more seemed to originate with the Democrats than the Republicans.

One that gained some traction was crafted by Professor Jacob Hacker of Yale, who proposed that employers either provide insurance for their workers or pay 6% of payroll to a new public insurance pool modeled on Medicare. This plan was the origin of the so-called public option that was much debated over the next several years. Critics resurrected familiar old worries about the loss of personal attention in a publicly-run system.

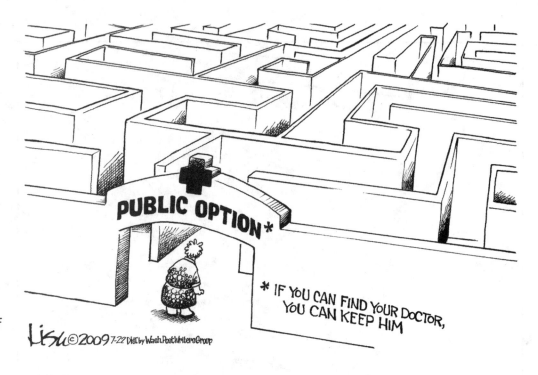

PUBLIC OPTION *

* IF YOU CAN FIND YOUR DOCTOR, YOU CAN KEEP HIM

Lisa © 2009 7-22 Dist by Wash.PostWritersGroup

Simultaneously Braking and Accelerating the HEALTH-CARE Vehicle

In February 2007 John Edwards tried to give a boost to his campaign for the Democratic presidential nomination by offering a health care plan much like the Massachusetts Plan but with a Medicare buy-in public option. Not all were impressed.

In September, presidential candidate Hillary Clinton offered a similar plan. This, too, drew critics.

She indicated that she had consulted with leading commercial health insurance and drug companies in order to get their buy-in, a move that Edwards condemned, but Clinton also suggested that she had learned from past political mistakes and now would give Congress a large input if she were elected. Clinton also proposed an individual mandate that everyone must have insurance. The individual mandate was originally an idea that was proposed by the conservative leaning Heritage Foundation in 1989 as an alternative to single-payer. It was included in several Republican alternative proposals from that time until recently. This mandate would later become a divisive issue as the health reform debate progressed, and many Republicans switched to opposing it.

Candidate Barack Obama had to play catch-up on the health reform issue and issued a plan similar to Edwards' and Clinton's but minus the individual mandate.

When Obama clinched the nomination, America's leading health insurers told him that they would accept his plan if he included an individual mandate. Many providers and others in the health industry remained skeptical.

Meanwhile, Republican candidate John McCain side-stepped the policy consensus with its multitiered, Massachusetts-Plan-like features and argued for a largely deregulated national insurance market. His idea attracted limited support.

Even before the November 2008 presidential election was decided, individual and organizational proponents of the consensus position were meeting with business and health care interest groups to work out a plan all could live with. Conservative Democrat Max Baucus, Chair of the Senate Finance Committee, anticipated an Obama victory by beginning to design legislation with bipartisan support. The Congressional Budget Office prepared for upcoming intense activity in early 2009 by adding health analysts to its staff. Eight days after Obama's victory, Baucus issued a white paper calling for a national insurance exchange. At the same time, leaders of American health insurance plans, business groups, and pharmaceutical companies announced their support of the emerging reform consensus. Most Republican politicians, however, backed away from health reform.

Obama's announcement that he would nominate former Senator and Majority Leader Tom Daschle, a long-time supporter of the consensus approach, to be Secretary of Health and Human Services signaled the nature of the anticipated reform legislation.

Although the President's reference to health reform in his Inaugural Address was vague in the extreme ("[We will] wield technology's wonders to raise health care's quality and lower its costs …"), it was apparent to Washington and health industry insiders that his administration was preparing to launch a major, centrist initiative in health reform.

5

The Quest for Obamacare

The Obama administration's efforts got off to a poor public start.

While Tom Daschle pursued quiet conversations with representatives of the health care industries, notably with former Congressman Billy Tauzin now representing the Pharmaceutical Research and Manufacturers of America (PhRMA), his nomination ran into trouble almost immediately.

Much negative talk circulated about his wife's role as a registered lobbyist for a big Washington firm with major health industry clients, and Daschle himself stumbled into a scandal over his failure to pay $140,000 in back taxes.

He withdrew his name from consideration for Secretary of the U.S. Department of Health and Human Services (DHHS) on February 3, 2009 and Obama chose Kathleen Sebelius, Governor of Kansas from 2003 to 2009 and a former state insurance commissioner, as his new nominee. She was formally nominated on March 2, 2009 — the same day Obama announced that Nancy-Ann DeParle was appointed Director of the White House Office of Health Reform and whose role was to take the public lead for the administration in health reform negotiations.

DeParle had run the Centers for Medicare and Medicaid Services (CMS), the agency that oversees Medicare and Medicaid, during the last three years of Clinton's administration, and then became managing director of a private equity firm while also serving as a board member of several companies including those in the health industry. Her appointment was positively received by industry leaders and drew praise from some Republicans. However, some were concerned that President Obama was getting too close to the industry.

Behind the scenes, the Obama administration was already engaging in intensive private negotiations with industry, with Rahm Emanuel, the President's chief of staff, taking the lead in his famously brusque and no-nonsense way. Emanuel was a veteran of the Clinton administration's failed reform efforts and took away from that experience the lesson that it was important to lower opposition to reform by finding pragmatic ways to deal with the special interests. His message to industry was a mixture of promise and threat, as he communicated his understanding that the new law would add millions of paying private customers (many with government subsidies) but if industry did not support the effort it could be subject to harsh regulation and deep cuts in the government's payments for its public programs, on which industry heavily depended.

Meanwhile, Senator Max Baucus and his Senate Finance Committee were given license to craft a bill to the administration's liking and also to be involved in direct negotiations with industry representatives.

The big public launch event was a health reform summit on March 5, 2009 in the East Room of the White House. It was attended by well over 100 people, including 50 members of Congress (Democrats and Republicans), leaders of organized labor, representatives of AARP, the Childrens' Defense Fund, and the Chamber of Commerce, representatives of the AMA and other professional organizations, corporate executives, Billy Tauzin of PhRMA, Karen Ignani representing the health insurance companies, and hospital representatives including Chip Kahn who had designed the original "Harry and Louise" commercials that helped sink the Clinton Administration's health reform proposal.

The cartoon contains the following text inside the speech bubble: "I MIGHT TAKE THE PUBLIC OPTION TURNPIKE. OR WE COULD CONSIDER THE CO-OP CAUSEWAY. BUT I'LL ALSO CONSIDER OTHER OPTIONS (DEPENDING ON OBSTACLES) OR WE COULD DO A U-TURN AND HEAD IN A DIFFERENT DIRECTION. UNLESS YOU HAVE A BETTER IDEA." The label "MAP" appears in the cartoon.

Nancy-Ann DeParle attended and was described as the administration's "health care czar" and the "point person" for reform efforts, although it was clear that Senator Baucus, also present, wanted to play a leading role in writing health care legislation. Senator Kennedy was expected to be a major player; in the House of Representatives, Speaker Nancy Pelosi would be a force as well. President Obama positioned himself as the "Mediator-in-Chief" and chose to present principles for health reform but did not submit an administration bill.

Secret discussions took place all spring between Baucus' aides, DeParle, and health industry representatives.

I'M GOING TO CANADA FOR THE CHEAP DRUGS.

THEN   NOW

The essence of the deal that got hammered out behind closed doors was incremental extension of Medicaid and SCHIP for low-income populations, and an individual mandate to require previously uninsured populations to purchase privately provided insurance marketed via a national insurance exchange. It included piecemeal fixes such as less stringent regulations on hospitals than the industry feared, and an agreement to improve Medicare, Part D. The possibility of single-payer ("Medicare for All") was completely bypassed.

The emerging plan did not allow the import of cheaper drugs from Canada and Europe or the use of federal bargaining power directly with pharmaceutical companies, to the disappointment of many patient advocates who wanted that leverage to help drive down the costs of medications.

I'D FEEL A LOT BETTER IF THE GUY IN FRONT WOULD STOP YELLING "WHEEEEEEE!"

PHARMACEUTICAL COMPANIES

HEALTH CARE COSTS

In exchange, the health care industries agreed to ramp down health cost inflation by some hundreds of billions over ten years, and PhRMA pledged to spend $200 million to advertise the advantages of reform.

Senator Baucus released a draft proposal for health reform on May 1 and his Finance Committee scheduled public hearings for select invitees. The hearings did not go as well as Baucus and the administration had hoped, however, and led instead to an embarrassing exposure of the industry-favoring bias of the legislation-in-process.

HEALTH CARE REFORM STALLS IN CONGRESS

I'M JUST NOT SEEING ANY GOOD SOLUTIONS.

HEALTH INC.

DRUG LOBBY

INSURANCE LOBBY

SINGLE PAYER

M.WUERKER POLITICO ©2009 Matt Wuerker.

The issues became clearest when strong single-payer supporters representing the Physicians for a National Health Program and other advocacy organizations protested their exclusion from the committee proceedings and demanded to be heard. Instead, on May 5, eight were arrested at the Senate Finance Committee hearings and immediately became known as the "Baucus 8." The events were widely reported by the media, the "Baucus 8" were acclaimed as heroes by many, and their pro-single-payer position was enthusiastically supported by liberal and progressive commentators.

To make matters worse for Baucus, his hopes for bipartisanship within his committee evaporated because Republican Senators Charles Grassley, Orrin Hatch, and others he was counting on became increasingly unwilling to fall out of step with their party as they shifted sharply to the right and against health reform.

The Obama administration grew impatient with Baucus because of the delay in the Senate, but it had far more serious problems with Democrats in the House, who were deeply factionalized and, to some extent, in open rebellion.

Approximately 60 Democratic representatives, like Dennis Kucinich and John Conyers, leaned strongly to the left and still preferred a single-payer option, while about an equal number were centrist and conservative "Blue Dogs" who objected even to the weaker "public option" alternative for the projected health insurance exchanges that House leadership now offered. The public option was the concept that a government public health plan similar to Medicare would be an available choice alongside private health plans for the uninsured in the proposed health exchanges. Many believed these plans would be more cost efficient and therefore more affordable than the private plans.

The Blue Dogs, like the Republicans, feared a public option would compete unfairly with the private insurance plans in the exchanges and pave the road to "socialism."

House Speaker and Democratic majority leader Nancy Pelosi had a difficult time gaining control over her own caucus, especially when powerful long-time liberal chair of the House Committee on Energy and Commerce Henry Waxman developed legislation of his own without paying heed to what was emerging from the Senate.

The political situation grew progressively worse for the Democrats during the summer of 2009, which saw a concerted right-wing attack on health care reform.

Reactionary media pundits and conservative Republican spokesmen led the assault with allusions to socialized medicine and a vast, centralized, impersonal government health bureaucracy, neither of which bore any resemblance to the details of health reform actually being proposed by the Obama administration and their representatives.

"YOU'VE GOT A PRE-EXISTING CONDITION."

Rick Scott, who resigned in 1997 as CEO of Columbia/HCA, the largest for-profit hospital chain in the country, amid charges of Medicare fraud, fueled much of this orchestrated attack through an organization called Conservatives for Patients' Rights. Similarly, billionaires Charles and David Koch created Patients United Now as another front organization for the right-wing antireform agenda.

In this climate and with this sort of backing, former Republican Majority Leader Dick Armey helped create the Tea Party Patriots, who then became the myopic shock troops in the battles against the Democrats' health reform plans.

Much of the Tea Party organizing was done in June and July for planned ambushes of Democratic legislators at their August town meetings, which frequently turned into angry shouting matches and near riots.

Unfortunately, the town hall meeting was taken over by the village idiots.

95

The opposition dubbed the legislation "Obamacare" as a repugnant term. Initially, the President and his staff tried to avoid the label, but later adopted it as a badge of honor saying, "Yes, President Obama cares."

One of the issues most shouted about were the so-called death panels allegedly included in the health reform legislation. This framing was actually a gross distortion of a forward-thinking proposal to reimburse providers for end-of-life counseling, an idea that many physicians thought would lead to better patient-centered care while potentially lowering costs.

Why Private Health Care is Better

The political situation got even worse for the Democrats when the press published revelations of the Obama administration's deals with industry. The shock and anger of progressive Democrats about the deal with PhRMA was captured by Henry Waxman who said, "We were never part of that deal. We are not bound by that deal."

ORGANIZER-IN-CHIEF

Liberal commentator Robert Reich, who had been Secretary of Labor in the Clinton administration, condemned the deal as "an assault on democracy." Later in August, the Obama administration was hit by a renewed and engineered assault from the right.

America's Health Insurance Plans (AHIP), the organization representing the health insurance industry, paid the Chamber of Commerce $86.2 million to mount a campaign against the developing health care legislation, especially against the provisions for the public option. One of the industry giants, United Health Care, encouraged its employees to join the Tea Party.

Soon, President Obama made statements that seemed to indicate that he was willing to concede to the health insurers by suggesting that the public option may have become "expendable."

The Precipice

This apparent cave-in came at the height of broad frustration with the administration on the part of liberals, who felt bitter disappointment because of the gap between Obama's rhetoric about "change" as a candidate and his Washington, deal-making, business-as-usual behavior in office.

In September, Obama tried to rally support for his administration's health reform efforts in a nationally televised speech to a joint session of Congress in which he said "I am not the first president to take up this cause, but I am determined to be the last."

National support for health reform rallied somewhat, but then a smooth transit to a quickly closed deal fell flat.

Nancy Pelosi had to address the concerns of antiabortion legislators in the House when conservative Democrat Bart Stupak of Michigan introduced an amendment to the health reform legislation that banned the coverage of abortion in essentially all insurance plans provided through the proposed national health care exchange.

Facing great outrage from liberal Democrats including the strong prochoice caucus to which she herself belonged, Pelosi struck the "ultimate" deal and forced through a vote on the amended legislation. It barely passed, 220 to 215, with 39 Democrats, mostly Blue Dogs, voting *No* and one Republican voting *Yes*.

In the Senate, there were several major roadblocks starting with Max Baucus, who voted against the public option in the Finance Committee he chaired, which meant that the option was missing from the legislation coming to the floor.

Other barriers were conservative Democrat Ben Nelson of North Dakota and former Democrat Joseph Lieberman of Connecticut, who both withheld their approval of the bill. Nelson objected to legislative language that he alleged favored abortion and because he claimed that the new law would impose undue Medicaid expenses on his state. Lieberman said he still feared the public option while his critics claimed that he was simply serving as a shill for the 72 private insurance companies based in his state.

The "hostage" situation in the Senate was particularly tense because the Democrats needed both Nelson's and Lieberman's votes to get the 60 required to prevent a Republican filibuster.

Matt Wuerker

Politico

Senate Democratic Majority Leader Harry Reid tried various maneuvers, including an embarrassing special deal for Nelson and a short-lived plan to allow buy-in to Medicare for those 55–64 as a political substitute for the public option.

When that collapsed too, liberals everywhere were outraged, and former Vermont Governor Howard Dean, Chair of the Democratic National Committee from 2005 to 2009, appeared on morning television shows urging Democrats to "kill the bill." He claimed that the legislation in its gutted form was "a bigger bailout for the insurance industry than [the bailout of] AIG." Outspoken liberal TV commentator Keith Olberman was among the many on the left who also urged the Senate to kill the bill and start over.

Eventually politics won the day, and the Senate passed the deeply compromised measure on Christmas Eve, 2009 by a strict party line vote of 60–40, including Nelson and Lieberman among the 60.

115

But going into 2010, Nancy Pelosi still claimed that she could not guarantee that the House Democrats would support health reform legislation which did not include a public option.

The Wake-Up Call

Yet another blow to the Democrats' quest was Republican Scott Brown's surprising victory over the Democratic candidate Martha Coakley in the January 19 special election to fill the Senate seat in Massachusetts vacated by Ted Kennedy's death.

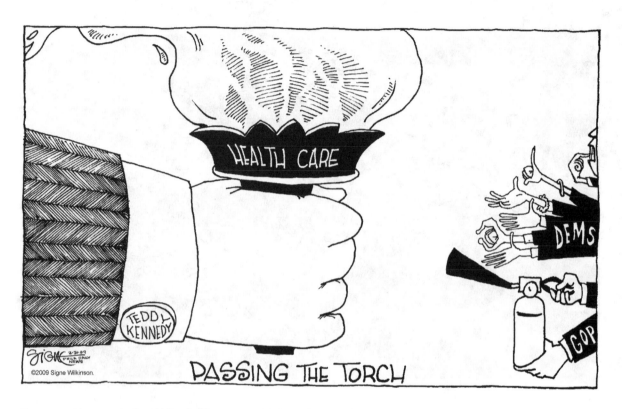

PASSING THE TORCH

Senator Kennedy had died of cancer on August 25, 2009. Not only did the Democrats and the nation lose one of health reform's biggest advocates, but Kennedy would have been the desperately needed 60th vote in the Senate for health reform. Many believe that had he been healthy and survived, a bill with more bipartisan support may have been possible. However, others believed that the political environment had become far too partisan for broad compromise.

In any case, Brown's victory caused great concern because the Senate Democrats could no longer count on the 60 votes necessary to ensure passage and Republicans believed that they had the votes to kill health reform.

President Obama was determined to revive the health reform effort despite lack of Republican spark.

With tremendous pressure from the White House …

....and through around-the-clock negotiating sessions and one-on-one arm-twisting, a final political deal was worked out that brought on board all Senate Democrats. The deal required the House Democrats to give up on the public option in their bill while the Senate would shift its bill from a national insurance exchange to state-based exchanges with a federal exchange as the default option if a state failed to act.

The final deal involved a compromise between the House and Senate bills via carefully timed legislative acrobatics. The House Democrats would vote to accept the Senate version of the legislation but would then amend it to include changes that were supposedly budget-related. Democrats in the Senate had already agreed in advance to pass the House version of the bill as a budget reconciliation measure, which only required a 51-vote majority.

The Senate Arrival

garyvarvel.com

Many political observers thought that the circus routine was more inept than smoothly executed and liberal Democrats in the House had great difficulties with the political maneuvers, especially now that single-payer was long gone and the public option had been recently jettisoned. The final vote in the House came on March 21, 2010, when the measure passed 219–212 with no Republican joining the Democrats.

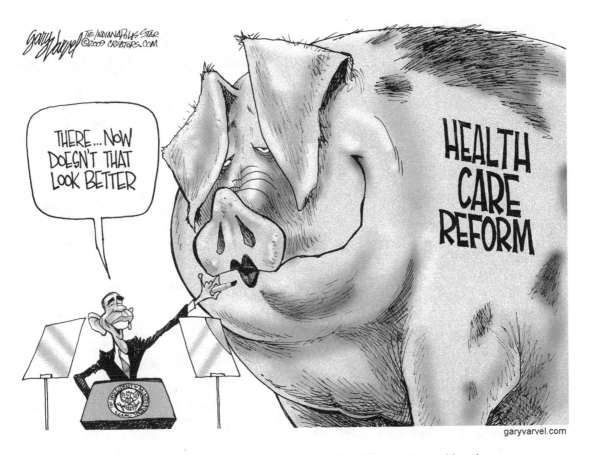

The Patient Protection and Affordable Care Act of 2010 was signed by the
President on March 23, and on March 25 both the House and Senate enacted
the prearranged reconciliation measure. The Obama administration had gotten
a reform bill passed, but it was viewed by many as deeply flawed legislation
that had come at great political cost.

6

The Aftermath

The Patient Protection and Affordable Care Act (ACA) of March 2010 was the clearly recognizable product of the political process that created it. The long and very complicated legislation lacks a simple coherence and is, instead, a multilayered composite of regulations, public insurance expansions, mandates, subsidies to help purchase private insurance, and incentives for system improvement that affect different groups of people at different times.

The law's provisions also roll out over several years, and it is widely believed that stepwise roll-out was built in to help lessen expected political opposition and to reduce the 10-year price tag. In many of its features ACA also reflects the special deals, last minute compromises, and ad hoc arrangements that were essential to securing Congressional approval.

The most central and controversial features are a large expansion of Medicaid and a set of mandates for employers and individuals to provide or purchase health insurance, a prospective marketplace mechanism of exchanges for buying and selling new insurance policies, and a set of government-financed subsidies to help people purchase mandated insurance — all of which are supposed to begin in 2014.

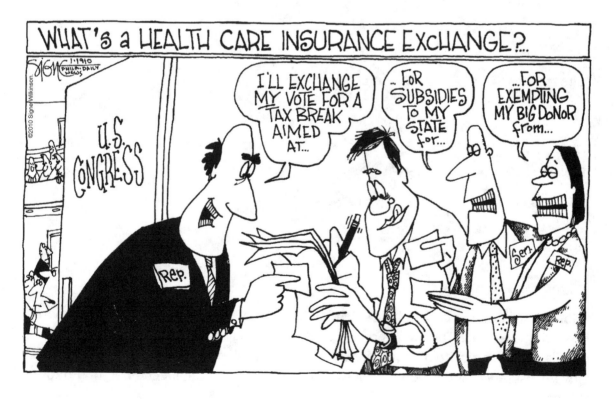

While the individual mandate requires that everyone without insurance buy it, nowhere is a right to health care guaranteed. Those with private coverage are assured certain new restrictions on the behavior of insurance companies, and some were implemented as early as 2010. Skeptics remarked that the only "right" truly guaranteed by ACA is granted to health insurers — to a significantly increased number of government-subsidized customers.

"IT'S A REMINDER OF WHAT WE CAN DO WHEN WE ALL WORK TOGETHER."

One view that seems to have achieved near universal consensus is that ACA more clearly reflects calculated pragmatism than idealism and has every appearance of being jerry-rigged.

Attacks on the Affordable Care Act began even before it was signed into law. Republicans in Congress complained bitterly that they had been "steam-rolled" and that the legislation had been rammed through with no conciliatory offers of negotiation or compromise.

In fact, ACA was the only major piece of domestic legislation in the history of the United States that passed on a strictly partisan basis. Unlike 1935, when a majority of Republican congressmen voted for Social Security despite their earlier opposition or 1965, when Medicare gained a majority of Republican votes in the House and a near even split of Republicans for and against in the Senate, ACA received not a single Republican vote in either chamber of Congress. Very likely in fear for their seats in conservative districts in the upcoming midterm elections, 34 Democrats also voted "Nay" along with the Republicans.

Bitterness quickly led to calls for legislative repeal.

Representative Paul Ryan (R-Wisconsin) announced that he looked "forward to the Republican party running on a platform of repealing the bill." While many questioned his motives, other Republicans, both in Congress and in state governments, vowed to challenge ACA in the federal courts.

Within days, several state attorneys general joined in a multistate lawsuit challenging ACA as unconstitutional on two grounds: (1) it mandated that individuals lacking insurance must purchase government-approved private insurance and (2) it called for a massive expansion of Medicaid. States were concerned about potential new costs at a time when their budgets were already in crisis from the recession. This is a complex and politically charged issue because the federal government would actually be picking up most of the costs for the expansion. Nevertheless, 26 states eventually joined this lawsuit, which was also joined in May 2010 by the National Federation of Independent Business.

The most visible and vociferous attacks — both political and legal — focused on the individual mandate, which supporters of ACA, health policy analysts, and insurance industry executives all agreed was an actuarial necessity and the irreplaceable centerpiece of the legislation.

BAR MITZVAH

OBAMITZVAH

Several provisions of ACA took effect within months of its passage and pleased many people. Among them were stipulations that as of September 2010 insurers could no longer rescind coverage except in cases of outright fraud, deny coverage to children with preexisting conditions, or impose lifetime limits on benefits. Also popular were more generous coverage for childhood immunizations and certain adult preventive services and a new allowance for parents to keep adult children on their policies until their 26th birthday.

ASK YOUR DOCTOR ABOUT ObamaCare®*

* Side effects include delayed treatment, elevated taxes, swelled deficits, shortages of doctors, and in some cases...DEATH.

ObamaCare 2 TRILLION mg

Lisa© 2009 6-11 Dist by Wash.PostWritersGroup

ACA also created a public health and prevention fund which will eventually add $2 billion of needed resources above existing appropriations, as well as a host of other prevention and wellness provisions. While popular with most health groups, the prevention fund has repeatedly come under attack by conservatives who do not support many of the population-based programs that the fund is designed to implement.

Several provisions offered new help to those on Medicare: everyone with Part D would receive a $250 rebate on drug costs for 2011, and the "donut hole" would gradually shrink over ten years. Moreover, Medicare would stop charging copays and deductibles for preventive services and would cover beneficiaries for annual wellness visits. Yet, in national polls seniors showed little enthusiasm for ACA and most even thought that costs would increase and benefits decrease.

In the population at large, opinion was very mixed and deeply divided. Ambivalent or negative opinion was tied closely to uncertainty about what ACA would really do and the strong, persistent sense that it would lead to increased taxes and add greatly to the massive and growing national deficit — no matter what the President or the Congressional Budget Office said.

These fears were fed by the deep economic recession, the highest unemployment rate since the Great Depression, and the persistent Republican effort to tie ACA to "job-killing and deficit-growing Obamacare."

The legal and political challenges to the Affordable
Care Act greatly intensified in the fall of 2010.
In Michigan, a federal judge ruled against the
argument that the ACA was unconstitutional, but in
Virginia a judge refused to dismiss the case.

In the U.S. District Court in the Northern District of Florida the judge put the multistate case involving Florida and 25 other states on his docket and ruled that Congress had exceeded its constitutional authority by requiring that, as of 2014, U.S. citizens purchase government-approved private health insurance (the individual mandate).

The fall elections at both the congressional and state levels were approached by many candidates as a referendum on ACA. Several Democrats worried that they would be made more vulnerable by their continued support.

Pledges to repeal or undermine ACA sparked many Republican campaigns.

The Democrats held on to a slim majority in the Senate but lost 63 seats in the House (the largest midterm loss since 1938), and many of the Democrats who held on did so in part because they jumped ship on the health care issue.

At the state level, Republicans won 29 governorships in 39 races and gained 680 seats in state legislatures. Many of the newly elected Republicans were strongly committed to repealing the ACA or, at the least, refusing to cooperate with its implementation at the state level, which was essential for the projected 2014 Medicaid expansion and set-up of insurance exchanges.

In November 2010 Florida's governor-elect, and former Columbia/HCA CEO Rick Scott, affirmed his intention to work for the repeal of the ACA, and after being inaugurated he refused federal money intended for the care of seniors, retirees, children, and the disabled and turned back planning money that was meant to assist the state in creating an insurance exchange. He and other Republican governors vowed to resist or sabotage the ACA in other ways as well, as by suspending, drastically cutting back or privatizing Medicaid.

In Congress, the Republicans committed themselves to massive cuts in social programs, allegedly to balance the budget and reduce the federal deficit. It was clear that the two parties had very different views on cost cutting.

New House majority leader John Boehner and Congressman Paul Ryan led the way, vowing to repeal the ACA and cut entitlement programs like Medicare.

Ryan's assault on Medicare by pushing for a much stingier and privatizing voucher system infuriated many, not least senior citizens, who saw his voucher proposal as a dangerous alternative to the protective security of Medicare.

The Good Deed

The Affordable Care Act also played a major role in the Republican presidential campaign, which gained considerable momentum by spring 2012. In the early primaries, the many candidates attempted to win votes by attacking Obamacare. Several made silly and historically unsupportable claims, such as Rick Santorum, who said that troops landed on the beach at Normandy during World War II to defend their private health insurance plans and resist earlier versions of Obamacare.

The candidate who emerged as the clear front runner and presumptive nominee, Mitt Romney, had to struggle with a confounding political problem. He denounced Obamacare along with the rest of the candidates in the Republican field.

But it was widely known to Romney's opponents that the health reform he had supported while governor of Massachusetts, "Romneycare," still hung like an albatross around his neck.

To many it was clear that Romneycare bore a striking resemblance in all essentials to Obamacare. The Affordable Care Act seemed to be Romney's baby, and its paternity was now a considerable embarrassment to the candidate.

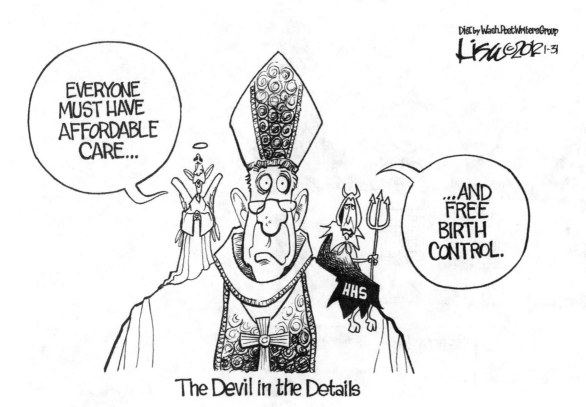

EVERYONE MUST HAVE AFFORDABLE CARE...

...AND FREE BIRTH CONTROL.

HHS

Dist by Wash.PostWritersGroup

Lisa ©2012 1-31

The Devil in the Details

President Obama had also been gearing up for the fall presidential election, but his campaign hit some major bumps besides the persistently poor state of the economy and disappointing employment statistics. The first of these was the birth control controversy that erupted in early February 2012. In January, the Obama administration announced that the ACA would require insurance plans at religious institutions to cover birth control without copayment for employees and perhaps students.

The administration relied on the recommendations of the prestigious Institute of Medicine, which based its advice on carefully considered evidence suggesting the value of birth control as a medically necessary preventive intervention "to ensure women's health and well-being." Catholic institutions protested immediately, invoking strong moral and religious objections.

Then the Republican presidential candidates jumped into the fray, alleging attacks on religious freedom by the Obama administration. A spokesperson for Mitt Romney said, "This is a direct attack on religious liberty and will not stand in a Romney presidency." Catholic leaders discovered , to their surprise in many cases, that their parishioners were often strongly in favor of the administration's position and not theirs.

Ever conscious of his political standing, President Obama, however, opted for a compromise that would allow employees of religious organizations that had religious objections to providing contraceptive services to obtain them with no cost-sharing.

DHHS Secretary Kathleen Sebelius announced in March that the contraceptive drugs and devices normally to be paid for by employers under the ACA could in these special cases be provided instead by pharmaceutical companies as special rebates or by one or more specially designated private insurers. The controversy gradually subsided but did not disappear entirely.

Probably the largest issue looming over the political landscape in the spring and early summer of 2012 was the impending decision of the Supreme Court on the constitutionality of the Affordable Care Act, particularly its provisions regarding the individual mandate and the requirement of states to comply with the dramatic expansion of Medicaid. Because of the variety and inconsistency of lower court rulings on these matters, the case was put on the Supreme Court's docket. The Obama administration welcomed the opportunity to establish the constitutionality of the ACA and submitted a long legal brief while claiming confidence about the positive outcome of the Court's review. Nonetheless, there was considerable trepidation in many quarters that the Court would undermine health reform's legal foundations and reverse whatever progress the ACA had achieved.

Many worried that this particular Supreme Court would be biased against the law and towards a more corporate friendly approach. They cited a series of recent rulings including the Citizens United *vs* the Federal Elections Commission case, which in effect allowed unlimited political donations as a manifestation of "free speech" by corporations. Some even suspected a Court bias towards Tea Party perspectives.

A New York Times/CBS News poll in June revealed that three-quarters of those polled believed that the Supreme Court's decisions are sometimes influenced by personal or political views. Others pointed out that the Court was sharply divided between conservative and liberal justices, with Justice Anthony Kennedy as the possibly pivotal vote on the ACA case.

The Solicitor General presented the Obama administration's case and tried to respond to sharp questioning from the bench in three days of argument in late March. On the second day of those hearings, on March 27, Justice Scalia asked, "May failure to purchase something subject me to regulation?" and Chief Justice Roberts asked whether the government could compel the purchase of cell phones.

Despite outward calm as it prepared for the announcement of the Court's decision in late June, the Obama administration appeared to be waiting with considerable trepidation.

In anticipation of possible Supreme Court decisions, intensive strategizing got under way in mid-June on all sides of the health reform issue. House Republican leaders planned to force an immediate vote on repeal if the ACA was not struck down in its entirety, and the Republican National Committee, in close consultation with Mitt Romney, geared up for a national drive for repeal. On the Democratic side, congressional representatives started carrying a card of talking points spelling out how many people the law has already helped — 86 million who have received free preventive care, 17 million children who can no longer be denied coverage because of preexisting conditions, and so on. The health insurance industry began a well orchestrated lobbying campaign called "The Link," which focused on advertising the essential connection between the individual mandate and new insurance regulations, making the case that if the individual mandate goes down so would the exclusion of preexisting conditions and other such popular measures.

Also noteworthy was the strategy pursued by advocates of a single-payer system. They viewed the impending Court decision, which they believed might strike down ACA in whole or part, as an opportunity to reenergize their campaign for "Medicare for All." They pointed out that during the Supreme Court hearings in March, liberal justices in their pointed questioning of attorneys opposing the individual mandate, indicated that they believed a Medicare-like system would be unassailably constitutional because, as Justice Sotomayor put it, "Congress can tax everybody and set up a public health care system." The questioned attorney responded that, "Yes, tax power is OK." Also, Justice Kennedy in his questioning said, "Let's assume that [Congress] could use the tax power to raise revenue and to just have a national health service, single payer" and then noted that this tax power would be clearly constitutional. The tax question actually played an even bigger role in the final decision than anyone imagined. In retrospect, Chief Justice Roberts seemed to signal during oral argument what would later become his final position on the individual mandate. During questioning the Chief Justice queried whether the individual mandate was a tax and not a penalty. Some liberals began to hope that this focus on tax-based constitutionality might even draw in President Obama and Democratic leadership.

When the Court announced its decision on June 28 it came as a great surprise to almost everyone. As anticipated, the liberal justices (Breyer, Ginsburg, Kagan, Sotomayor) voted that the individual mandate was consitutional on the basis of the interstate commerce clause, but the conservative justices (Alito, Roberts, Scalia, Thomas) voted against it on this basis, with Kennedy joining the conservative side. But in an unanticipated move, Chief Justice Roberts, appointed to the Court under Republican President George W. Bush, declared that the individual mandate could stand because it was constitutional under the tax and spend power granted to Congress by the constitution .

Because the Affordable Care Act, as of 2014, would require uninsured individuals to purchase insurance or pay a penalty that would be collected by the Internal Revenue Service, Justice Roberts reasoned that this penalty was a tax and therefore a legitmate basis for the consitutionality of the individual mandate. The four liberal justices then joined Roberts for a 5-4 majority upholding the ACA.

Chattanooga Times Free Press **Bennett**

In the immediate aftermath of the decision, most Democrats rejoiced in what they took to be a victory and vindication of their tough fight to pass the ACA. But Republicans in Congress vowed to vote for an immediate repeal.

FINALLY, THE DEATH PANEL COMETH...

Thanks to Chief Justice Roberts, Republicans were armed with new rhetoric about what they now claimed were the tax-hike implications of Obamacare.

Political observers understood that any such vote would be a largely symbolic and grandstanding gesture because of the Democratic majority in the Senate and the certainty of a presidential veto if the repeal measure somehow survived in Congress. Presumptive Republican presidential candidate Mitt Romney also pledged to campain against "tax-raising Obamacare" and to rescind it immediately if elected.

Liberal Democrats and other progressives regrouped, and many of them made new commitments to push for a single-payer system with renewed vigor.

Temporarily overshadowed in the glare of the moment was the realization that the Supreme Court made another important decision crucial to the future of the Affordable Care Act. For poor people at or slightly above the federal poverty level, the ACA was supposed to provide health coverage by expanding Medicaid, beginning in 2014. The law provides generous federal subsidies for that expansion, but this part of health reform must be implemented at the state level. The states must therefore cooperate and provide certain financial resources of their own which many states have been claiming they do not have even with the prospect of generous new federal monies. The Court decided by the same 5-4 majority that upheld the individual mandate that the federal government could *encourage* states to expand their Medicaid rolls and to reward them financially for doing so, but by a 7-2 ruling (with only Ginsburg and Sotomayor in opposition) it also decided that the federal government *could not penalize* states that did not comply by withholding all federal Medicaid funds because such an action would be "coercive" and, thus, unconstitutional. In light of this ruling many states immediately indicated that they might not expand their Medicaid rolls because they could not afford to do so. If this becomes a widespread state reaction, millions of poor individuals who were expected to be covered under the Affordable Care Act will not, in fact, be covered.

State pushback combined with staunch Republican political opposition are merely two parts of the continuing struggle over the ACA, which the Supreme Court's decision in no way put to rest.

The battles are likely to continue long into the future. As Yogi Berra famously said, "It ain't over till it's over."

Abbreviations

AALL	American Association of Labor Legislation
AARP	American Association of Retired Persons
ACA	Affordable Care Act (full name: Patient Protection and Affordable Care Act of 2010)
AHIP	America's Health Insurance Plans
AIG	American International Group (an American multinational insurance company which was "bailed out" by the Federal Reserve Bank)
AMA	American Medical Association
ANA	American Nurses Association
APHA	American Public Health Association
CAP	Center for American Progress
CCMC	Committee on the Costs of Medical Care
CDC	Centers for Disease Control and Prevention
CMS	Centers for Medicare and Medicaid Services
Columbia/HCA	Large for-profit health company resulting from the merger in 1993 of Columbia Hospital Corporation and Hospital Corporation of America
DHHS	Department of Health and Human Services
HCCU	Health Care Coalition for the Uninsured
HIPAA	Health Insurance Portability and Accountability Act
HMO	Health Maintenance Organization
JAMA	Journal of the American Medical Association
MMA	Medicare Modernization Act of 2003
Part D	Prescription drug coverage plan for Medicare beneficiaries, included in the MMA
PhRMA	Pharmaceutical Research and Manufacturers of America
PNHP	Physicians for a National Health Program
SCHIP	State Children's Health Insurance Program

Suggestions for Further Reading

Anne-Emanuelle Birn, Theodore M. Brown, Elizabeth Fee, and Walter J. Lear, "Struggles for National Health Reform in the United States", **American Journal of Public Health:** 93.1 (January 2003): 86–91.

David Blumenthal and James A. Morone, **The Heart of Power: Health and Politics in the Oval Office** (Berkeley: University of California Press, 2009).

Karen Davis, **National Health Insurance: Benefits, Costs, and Consequences** (Washington, DC: The Brookings Institution, 1975).

Alan Derickson, **Health Security for All: Dreams of Universal Health Care in America** (Baltimore: Johns Hopkins University Press, 2005).

John P. Geyman, **Hijacked: The Road to Single Payer in the Aftermath of Stolen Health Care Reform** (Monroe, Maine: Common Courage Press, 2010).

Colin Gordon, **Dead on Arrival: The Politics of Health Care in Twentieth-Century America** (Princeton: Princeton University Press, 2003).

Beatrix Hoffman, **The Wages of Sickness: The Politics of Health Insurance in Progressive America** (Chapel Hill: University of North Carolina Press, 2001).

Theodore Marmor, **The Politics of Medicare,** Second Edition (New York: Aldine Transaction Publishers, 2000).

Ronald L. Numbers, **Almost persuaded: American physicians and compulsory health insurance, 1912–1920** (Baltimore: Johns Hopkins University Press, 1978).

Jonathan Oberlander, **The Political Life of Medicare** (Chicago: University of Chicago Press, 2003).

Jonathan Oberlander, "Long Time Coming: Why Health Reform Finally Passed," **Health Affairs, 29.6** (June 2010):1112–1116.

Jill Quadango, **One Nation, Uninsured: Why the U.S. Has No National Health Insurance** (New York: Oxford University Press, 2005).

Theda Skocpol, **Boomerang: Clinton's Health Security Effort and the Turn Against Government in U.S. Politics** (New York: Norton, 1996).

Paul Starr, **Remedy and Reaction: The Peculiar American Struggle over Health Care Reform** (New Haven: Yale University Press, 2011).

Paul Starr, **The Social Transformation of American Medicine** (New York: Basic Books, 1983).

Robert Stevens and Rosemary Stevens, **Welfare Medicine in America: A Case Study of Medicaid** (New York: Free Press, 1974).

Arthur Viseltear, "Emergence of the Medical Care Section of the American Public Health Association, 1926–1948," **American Journal of Public Health,** 63.11 (November 1973): 986–105.

Bruce Vladeck, "Universal Health Insurance in the United States: Reflections on the Past, the Present, and the Future" **American Journal of Public Health**, 93.1 (January 2003): 16–19.

Washington Post Staff, **Landmark: The Inside Story of America's New Health Care Law and What It Means for Us All** (New York: PublicAffairs, 2010).

Health Policies in the United States

Interested readers can view the entire original documents mentioned in this book online:

Compilation of the Social Security Laws, including the original Social Security Act of 1935, Medicare and Medicaid Acts (Titles 18 and 19) of 1965, the SCHIP extension, and the Medicare Modernization Act of 2003: http://www.ssa.gov/OP_Home/ssact/ssact.htm

The Social Security Documents and Amendments, including the original Social Security Act of 1935, and Medicare and Medicaid Amendments, are available with additional commentary and multimedia features via the National Archives website: http://www.archives.gov/ (use search button for specific documents)

Full text of the Affordable Care Act: http://www.healthcare.gov/law/full/

Merit and Amicus Briefs presented to the Supreme Court about the ACA, for Petitioners, Respondents, and Others: http://www.americanbar.org/publications/preview_home/11-393.html

Patient Protection and Affordable Care Act Opinion as decided on June 28, 2012 is available on the Supreme Court's website: http://www.supremecourt.gov/opinions/11pdf/11-393c3a2.pdf

Other related websites:

Policy Analysis, Research and Statistics:

Agency for Healthcare Research and Policy: http://www.ahrq.gov/

Commonwealth Foundation http://www.commonwealthfoundation.org/

Kaiser Family Foundation http://www.kff.org/

"Think Tanks":

Center for American Progress http://www.americanprogress.org/issues/domestic/healthcare/

Heritage Foundation http://www.heritage.org/initiatives/health-care

About the Authors

Georges C. Benjamin, MD, FACP, FACEP(E), FNAPA, Hon FRSPH, is the executive director of the American Public Health Association, the nation's oldest and largest organization of public health professionals. Previously, he was the secretary of the Maryland Department of Health and Mental Hygiene from 1999 - 2002 following four years as its deputy secretary for public health services. For the last 20 years he actively practiced public health at the local, state, and national levels with expertise in the areas of emergency preparedness, administration, and infectious diseases. Dr. Benjamin serves as publisher of the field's premier journal, the *American Journal of Public Health*, *The Nation's Health* newspaper, and the APHA's timeless publication on infectious diseases, the *Control of Communicable Diseases Manual*.

Dr. Benjamin is a graduate of the Illinois Institute of Technology and the University of Illinois, College of Medicine. He is board-certified in internal medicine and a fellow of the American College of Physicians. Also, he is a fellow emeritus of the American College of Emergency Physicians, an honorary fellow of the Royal Society of Public Health, a fellow of the National Academy of Public Administration, and a member of the Institute of Medicine of the National Academies.

Theodore M. Brown is Professor of History and of Community and Preventive Medicine and Medical Humanities at the University of Rochester. His research falls into several areas: the history of U.S. and international public health; the history of U.S. health policy and politics; and the history of psychosomatic medicine, "stress" research, and biopsychosocial approaches to clinical practice. He is a Contributing Editor (History) of the *American Journal of Public Health* and Editor of *Rochester Studies in Medical History*, a book series of the University of Rochester Press. He coedited and substantially coauthored *Making Medical History: The Life and Times of Henry E. Sigerist* (Johns Hopkins University Press, 1997) and, with Anne-Emanuelle Birn, recently completed an edited collection of essays, *Comrades in Health: American Health Internationalists, Abroad and at Home*, which will be published by Rutgers University Press. He is currently working with various collaborators on three other book projects.

Susan Ladwig has served as the Research and Quality Improvement Coordinator for the Palliative Care Program at the University of Rochester Medical Center since 2006. Her 2007 MPH thesis, "Who Uses Palliative Care: Characteristics of Inpatient Decedents and their Attending Physicians, " was presented at the 2008 meeting of the American Academy of Hospice and Palliative Medicine. She was first author of a report commissioned by the Upstate N.Y. Palliative Care Research Consortium, "Variations in End-of-Life

Care in New York State" and was an invited speaker at several conferences, including the Hospice and Palliative Care Association of New York State, to present this research. In addition, Susan is a contributing author for several other recently published and papers currently in-press in peer-reviewed journals including *Health Affairs, Journal of Pain and Symptom Management, Gerontologist, Patient Education & Counseling,* and *Journal of Palliative Medicine*. She reads cartoons and supports the "Medicare for All" movement whenever she can.

Elyse Berkman is a Masters of Public Administration Candidate at The City University of New York, Bernard M. Baruch College. After graduating from Syracuse University with a Bachelors of Fine Arts, Elyse moved to New York City, where she worked for a leading multinational textile development corporation designing textiles for home furnishings. Elyse hopes to transition to a career in health care policy after she graduates in 2013.

Index

Cartoonist and Publication Date

Anderson, Nick – Published originally in the Louisville Courier Journal*. All others published originally in the Houston Chronicle.

Pg. 36*	May 1, 1993		Pg. 47*	June 29, 2003
Pg. 84*	September 29, 2004		Pg. 55	September 27, 2007
Pg. 54	October 19, 2007		Pg. 83	June 17, 2009
Pg. 58	July 24, 2009		Pg. 57	August 7, 2009
Pg. 46	August 11, 2009		Pg. 82	August 23, 2009
Pg. 88*	November 20, 2009		Pg. 81	January 21, 2010
Pg. 81	February 24, 2010		Pg. 142	November 3, 2010
Pg. 45	January 20, 2011		Pg. 147	May 27, 2011
Pg. 167	June 29, 2012		Pg. 174	July 12, 2012

Babin, Rex - Published originally in the Sacramento Bee.

Pg. 160	January 26, 2011

Bell, Darin - "Candorville" published originally via the Washington Post Writers Group.

Pg. 33	January 19, 2006

Bennett, Clay – Published originally in Christian Science Motor*. All others published originally in the Chattanooga Times Free Press.

Pg. 44*	September 15, 1993		Pg. 67	February 9, 2008
Pg. 58	July 22, 2009		Pg. 102	July 25, 2009
Pg. 94	August 9, 2009		Pg. 69	September 13, 2009
Pg. 120	September 24, 2009		Pg. 109	October 17, 2009
Pg. 123	November 10, 2009		Pg. 64	November 19, 2009
Pg. 74	February 11, 2010		Pg. 131	March 23, 2010
Pg. 145	March 2, 2011		Pg. 149	April 5, 2012
Pg. 169	June 29, 2012			

Benson, Lisa – Published originally in the Victor Valley (CA) Press.

Pg. 71	February 13, 2008	Pg. 137	June 11, 2009
Pg. 70	July, 22, 2009	Pg. 113	November 24, 2009
Pg. 101	December 18, 2009	Pg. 144	January 22, 1010
Pg. 122	March 2, 2010	Pg. 66	April 13, 2010
Pg. 64	September 20, 2010	Pg. 135	December 15, 2010
Pg. 97	December 29, 2010	Pg. 132	January 17, 2011
Pg. 159	February 2, 2011	Pg. 140	October 18, 2011
Pg. 154	January 31, 2012	Pg. 163	March 30, 2012

Berryman, Clifford

| Pg. 13 | November 21, 1945 |

Block, Herb – Published originally via NEA Services*. All others published originally in the Washington Post.

Pg. 12*	July 27, 1938	Pg. 21	May 2, 1962
Pg. 24	July 4, 1963	Pg. 27	September 12, 1979
Pg. 34	May 3, 1991		

Bok, Chip – Published originally via Creators Syndicate.

Pg. 99	August 6, 2009	Pg. 116	August 20, 2009
Pg. 112	December 24, 2009	Pg. 106	March 22, 2010
Pg. 129	March 24, 2010	Pg. 152	March 30, 2010
Pg. 138	April 2, 2010	Pg. 89	December 20, 2010
Pg. 162	December 26, 2011	Pg. 168	June 28, 2012

Danziger, Jeff – Published originally via Cartoon Arts International/NY Times Syndicate.

| Pg. 97 | September 17, 2009 | Pg. 150 | June 8, 2011 |

Deering, John – Published originally in the Arkansas Democrat-Gazette.

Pg. 85	June 22, 2009	Pg. 72	June 20, 2009
Pg. 40	December 24, 2009	Pg. 79	January 27, 2010
Pg. 42	April 4, 2010		

Donnelly, Liza – Published originally via self-syndication.

| Pg. 62 | July 5, 2011 |

Judge, Lee – Published originally in the Kansas City Star.

| Pg. 92 | December 30, 2009 | Pg. 130 | March 16, 2010 |
| Pg. 133 | March 18, 2010 | | |

Kelley, Steve- Published originally in the Times-Picayune, New Orleans.

Pg. 49	December 3, 2003	Pg. 72	September 20, 2007
Pg. 101	September 11, 2009	Pg. 119	January 20, 2011
Pg. 68	December 1, 2011	Pg. 158	February 12, 2012
Pg. 166	June 29, 2012		

Lester, Mike – Published originally in the Rome (GA) News Tribune.

| Pg. 136 | August 2011 | Pg. 141 | June 2011 |

Luckovich, Mike – Published originally in the Atlanta Journal-Constitution.

Pg. 51	December 6, 2005	Pg. 78	February 2, 2009
Pg. 02	July 24, 2009	Pg. 108	August 28, 2009
Pg. 38	December 18, 2009	Pg. 41	March 4, 2010
Pg. 67	March 23, 2010	Pg. 153	March 25, 2010
Pg. 153	October 12, 2011	Pg. 156	February 2, 2012
Pg. 170	June 29, 2012		

May, Rex – Published originally via self-syndication.

| Pg. 44 | August 13, 2008 |

Peters, Mike – Published originally in the Dayton Daily News.

Pg. 39	June 15, 1993	Pg. 48	November 29, 2003
Pg. 84	October 27, 2006	Pg. 54	December 23, 2007
Pg. 157	August 14, 2009	Pg. 90	August 18, 2009
Pg. 100	September 8, 2009	Pg. 75	April 27, 2011
Pg. 43	February 8, 2012		

Pett, Joel - Published originally in USA Today*. All others published originally in the Lexington Herald-Leader.

Pg. 28	July 31, 2009	Pg. 115	August 18, 2009
Pg. 65	November 25, 2009	Pg. 105	March 16, 2010
Pg. 143	September 27, 2010*	Pg. 171	June 29, 2012

Piraro, Dan – "Bizarro" published originally via King Features Syndicate.
      Pg. 68   April 19, 2010

Poinier, Aurthur
      Pg. 23   May 2, 1961

Powell, Dwane – Published originally in the Raleigh News and Observer.
      Pg. 61   July 27, 2009   Pg. 107   September 21, 2009

Smith, Mike – Published originally in the Las Vegas Sun.
      Pg. 151   May 15, 2011   Pg. 164   July 13, 2012

Telnaes, Ann – Published originally via syndication.
      Pg. 59   May 16, 2006

Thaves, Bob and Tom –"Frank and Ernest" published originally via United Media/Universal Press.
      Pg. 34   May 31, 1995   Pg. 60   March 26, 2000
      Pg. 68   October 1, 2010   Pg. 37   December 6, 2011

Varvel, Gary – Published originally in the Indianapolis News*. All others published originally in the Indianapolis Star.

Pg. 35*	September 15, 1993	Pg. 77	February 23, 2009
Pg. 88	July 4, 2009	Pg. 121	July 22, 2009
Pg. 95	August 11, 2009	Pg. 125	September 9, 2009
Pg. 124	November 10, 2009	Pg. 83	January 6, 2010
Pg. 117	January 21, 2010	Pg. 139	March 15, 2010
Pg. 71	March 18, 2010	Pg. 119	January 9, 2011
Pg. 173	January 15, 2011	Pg. 138	January 26, 2011

Wilkinson, Signe – Published originally in the Philadelphia Daily News.

Pg. 63	June 27, 2001	Pg. 52	June 24, 2003
Pg. 50	November 3, 2005	Pg. 56	August 23, 2007
Pg. 73	September 20, 2007	Pg. 78	June 26, 2009
Pg. 118	August 31, 2009	Pg. 103	November 24, 2009
Pg. 128	January 19, 2010	Pg. 134	March 30, 2010

| Pg. 96 | January 7, 2011 | Pg. 155 | February 9, 2012 |
| Pg. 172 | July 1, 2012 | | |

Wuerker, Matt- Published originally via self-syndication*. All others published originally in Politico.

Pg. 105	March 23, 2005*	Pg. 148	March 23, 2005*
Pg. 73	October 6, 2008	Pg. 86	July 22, 2009
Pg. 87	July 30, 2009	Pg. 110	August 28, 2009
Pg. 165	September 1, 2009	Pg. 91	September 9, 2009
Pg. 80	September 21, 2009	Pg. 104	November 18, 2009
Pg. 114	December 21, 2009	Pg. 98	February 16, 2010
Pg. 87	February 25, 2010	Pg. 111	March 1, 2010
Pg. 131	March 23, 2010	Pg. 93	July 27, 2010
Pg. 146	January 18, 2011	Pg. 03	July 25, 2011
Pg. 127	March 13, 2012	Pg. 161	March 30, 2012

Image Credits